YEHUDA AMICHAI Selected Poems

T0322876

YEHUDA AMICHAI

Selected Poems

Edited by TED HUGHES *and*
DANIEL WEISSBORT

faber and faber

First published in 2000
by Faber & Faber Ltd
The Bindery
51 Hatton Garden
London ECIN 8HN

This edition first published in 2018

Photoset by Wilmaset Ltd, Birkenhead, Wirral
Printed in the UK by Imprint Digital, Exeter

A CIP record for this book
is available from the British Library

ISBN 978-0-571-35338-5

Our authorised representative in the EU for product safety is
Easy Access System Europe, Mustamäe tee 50, 10621 Tallinn, Estonia
gpsr.requests@easproject.com

10 9

Contents

List of Translators

GA	Glenda Abramson
AB	Abraham Birman
CB	Chana Bloch
RF	Robert Friend
AG	Assia Gutmann
BH/BH	Benjamin and Barbara Harshav
TH	Ted Hughes
CK	Chana Kornfeldt
SM	Stephen Mitchell
TP	Tudor Parfitt
HS	Harold Schimmel
DS	Dennis Silk

Introduction TED HUGHES

You ask me my opinion of what distinguishes Yehuda as a poet.

Whatever it is, it makes him to my mind one of the most interesting and rewarding poets alive.

I see his differentness on three levels. First there's the 'shared' differentness of his generation of poets. In England, in the early sixties, we suddenly became aware of new translations of poetry produced by writers of Eastern and Western Europe who came of age during the war – roughly the 1920s generation. This poetry seemed to us so absolutely new, so real, and excited us so much, that Daniel Weissbort and myself launched a magazine simply to make it available in English. So the first issue contained poems by (among others) Zbigniew Herbert, Miroslav Holub, Vasko Popa and Yehuda Amichai. It had been Daniel Weissbort's latest discovery – the Amichai – that decided us to go ahead.

That magazine, *Modern Poetry in Translation*, is still going, but after nearly thirty years, after thousands of contemporary poems translated from many languages, hundreds of new names, the monuments that have survived best, the massifs that have loomed continually bigger and more central, were in that first issue. It seems clear enough, now, that they belonged to the last – the most recent – 'great' generation of poets. And those four names have gradually moved into the foreground among the half dozen crucial figures.

They were starkly different from anything before and from anything since. Their differentness was a matter of recognizably 'great' qualities – something to do with their first-hand experience of, and response to, that mid-century cataclysm. One ability that they had in common worked to their advantage. Each one invented a poetic language of metaphor – a picture language – that operates clearly and powerfully behind the surface texture of the words. This picture language survives translation in the most extraordinary way. It is hard to imagine that many of Yehuda's poems can be better in Hebrew than they are in English. And I am told they go into Chinese just as easily. But one other characteristic that these poets shared was even more significant. Each one seemed to speak for a whole people at that most abnormal moment in their history. In those languages, with no shortage of brilliant talents, no other poet since has managed anything like it.

Saying that makes the second difference clear – Amichai's difference from Holub, Popa, Herbert and their coevals. Behind each of them, obviously, is their own national history – behind Popa the internal and external history of the Balkan peoples, the Serbs in particular, behind Herbert that of Poland, behind Holub that of Czechoslovakia – but behind Amichai the internal and external history of the Jews of modern Israel. One component of that Jewish history – the biblical component – already sets him in a wholly different category from the others. It sets his imagination in a vastly different mythic and historical order, one that is also a more universal order – to some degree shared by all peoples touched by the Bible. This might not be so significant if Amichai's secular imagination had not taken over, with such a rich comprehensive grasp, that huge inner stage and props and drama of Jewish sacred history, to perform his parables of the modern multi-cultural world and the present moment.

But speaking for his generation of Israelis, as from our perspective he seems to do, has given him responsibilities that are even bigger and certainly unique. He found a voice not just for a people in crisis but for the resurrection of a people, an ancient people, which was simultaneously the creation of a new people – what was simultaneously that people's emergence as central character in a global political drama at the crux of two deadlocked civilizations. These attributes are not fanciful: you can trace them like inflamed nerves everywhere in his poems – from the early 'United Nations Command in Jerusalem' to 'Temporary Poem of my Time' in his 1991 book *Even a Fist Was Once an Open Palm With Fingers*.

Those two categories of 'difference' are the back of the carpet. The third category is the one that turns them to account. His actual voice, his mental play, the verbal concoction that he offers the reader. One could analyse this at infinite length, and it has been analysed often enough. Again, trying to be simple, I see two main currents – the play of his metaphor or rather his worlds of experience and wisdom on the one hand and, on the other, oceanic feeling, the feeling he wields in the play of his metaphor and in the tone of his voice, the big music that accompanies his play. Whatever these two combined amount to, they make him the poet whose books I still open most often, most often take on a journey, most often return to when the whole business of writing anything natural, real and satisfying, seems impossible. And that after thirty years of feeling the same way about him. The effect his poetry has on me is to give me my own life – to open it up somehow, to make it all available to me afresh, to uncover all kinds of riches in every moment of

it, and to free me from my mental prisons. When that's
what I want, I pick up a book by Yehuda.

NOTE BY D.W.
These remarks by Ted Hughes were sent to me by him for possible
use in the collection of Amichai's work that we were planning. The
circumstances of their composition are not clear, but although Ted
Hughes would probably have rewritten them before committing them
to print, it seems appropriate to print them here for the first time as
an introduction to the present volume.

Selected Poems

A Bride without Dowry

A bride without dowry with a deep navel
In her tanned belly. A little hole
For food and drink, for birds.

Oh, yes, this is the bride with her big buttocks
Surprised out of her dreams and her fat
In which she had bathed naked
Like Susanna and the Elders.

Oh, yes, this is this serious girl
With freckles. What's the meaning
Of an upper lip pushing itself over the lower!
Dark drinking and laughter,
Little sweet animal, Monique.

And she has a will of iron
Inside a body of soft and spoiled flesh:
What a terrible blood bath
Is she preparing for herself,
What a terrible Roman arena streaming with blood.

[YA / TH]

A Child Is Something Else Again

A child is something else again. Wakes up
in the afternoon and in an instant he's full of words,
in an instant he's humming, in an instant warm,
instant light, instant darkness.

A child is Job. They've already placed their bets on him
but he doesn't know it. He scratches his body
for pleasure. Nothing hurts yet.

They're training him to be a polite Job,
to say 'Thank you' when the Lord has given,
to say 'You're welcome' when the Lord has taken away.

A child is vengeance.
A child is a missile into the coming generations.
I launched him: I'm still trembling.

A child is something else again: on a rainy spring day
glimpsing the Garden of Eden through the fence,
kissing him in his sleep,
hearing footsteps in the wet pine needles.
A child delivers you from death.
Child, Garden, Rain, Fate.

[CB]

End of Summer Evening in Motsa

A long bulldozer fights with his hill
Like a poet, like all who work here alone.
A heavy lust of ripe figs
Pulls the evening's ceiling to the level of the earth.
Fire has already eaten the thorns
And death won't have to do a thing except
Fold up like disappointed flames.
I can be consoled: a great love
Can also be a love for landscape.
A deep love for wells, a burning for olive-trees,
Or digging like bulldozers alone.

My thoughts are always polishing my childhood
Till it's become like a hard diamond,

Unbreakable, to cut
Into the cheap glass of my maturity.

[HS]

A Mutual Lullaby

A long time ago I wanted to tell you to sleep.
But your eyes won't let sleep come; your thighs won't,
Your belly, which I touch, perhaps.
So count backward as for launching a spacecraft,
And sleep, or count forward
As to start a song, and sleep.

Let's make sweet eulogies for each other
While we lie together in the dark. Tears
Remain longer than what caused them.
The newspaper was burned to a mist
By my eyes and the wheat
Goes on growing in Pharaoh's dream.
Time is not inside the clock
And love is, sometimes, in bodies.
Words you utter out of your sleep
Are food and drink for the wild angels.
And our dishevelled bed
Is the last nature reserve,
With screaming laughter and green, fat weeping.

A long time ago I wanted to tell you to sleep
And that the black night will be upholstered
With red soft velvet around all that's
Hard in you, like a case
Of geometrical instruments.

And that I shall keep you sacred like the Sabbath,
Also during working days, and that
We shall always stay together
Just as on a Happy New Year card
With a dove and the Holy Scroll
Covered with silver dust.
And that we are still cheaper
Than a computer. And that's why they'll
Not mind if we go on living.

[YA / TH]

A Man Doesn't Have Time

A man doesn't have time
to have time for everything.
He doesn't have seasons enough to have
a season for every purpose. Ecclesiastes
was wrong about that.

A man needs to love and to hate at the same moment,
to laugh and cry with the same eyes,
with the same hands to cast away stones and to gather
    them,
to make love in war and war in love.

And to hate and forgive and remember and forget,
to set in order and confuse, to eat and to digest
what history
takes years and years to do.

A man doesn't have time.
When he loses he seeks, when he finds
he forgets, when he forgets he loves, when he loves
he begins to forget.

And his soul is experienced, his soul
is very professional.
Only his body remains forever .
an amateur. It tires and it misses,
gets muddled, doesn't learn a thing,
drunk and blind in its pleasures
and in its pains.

He will die as figs die in autumn,
shrivelled and full of himself and sweet,
the leaves growing dry on the ground,
the bare branches already pointing to the place
where there's time for everything.

[CB]

A Snare Flies Up

A snare flies up from the ground
with outspread wings, this summer night.

A computer rolls his eyes upward
like a happy martyred saint.

Hoarse girls lure men
to their outing with hoarse voices.

In a lighted house sweet lovers tear
each other to quiet blood-dripping rags.

In the garages of the Kidron Valley
a black hearse is being repaired.

An orphaned father seats his little son on his knees
and sings him a lullaby about his sins.

The eyes of the sleepers are mines,
the first light of day will set them off.

[YA / TH]

To a Convert

A son of Abraham is studying to be a Jew.
He wants to be a Jew in no time at all.
Do you know what you're doing?
What's the hurry? After all, a man isn't
a fig tree: everything all at once, leaves and fruit
at the same time. (Even if the fig tree is
a Jewish tree.)

Aren't you afraid of the pain of circumcision?
Don't you worry that they'll cut and cut
till there's nothing left of you
but sweet Jew pain?

I know: you want to be a baby again,
to be carried around on an embroidered cushion, to be
    handed
from woman to woman, mothers and godmothers
with their heavy breasts and their wombs. You want the
    scent
of perfume in your nostrils, and wine
for your little smacking lips.

Now you're in the hospital. You're resting, recovering.
Women are waiting under the window for your foreskin.
Whoever catches it – you'll be hers, hers, hers.

[CB]

A Sweet Color Picture

A sweet color picture of plowman and horse from the
    turn of the century
on one of those early collective farms in Palestine
hanging on the wall of a summer home in a land far away
    across the sea.
And around that house, a luxurious lawn
hedged about with flowers, and on the lawn, an empty
    chair.
And I said unto myself: Sit down on this chair, sit and
    remember,
sit and judge – otherwise, some other person will sit here
to remember and to judge. What took place an hour ago
had its place, and what took place on that farm at the
    turn of the century
had its place, and there were trees whose leaves blustered
    in the wind
and trees that stood by silently. And the wind
the same wind. And the bluster and the silence in the
    trees.
And what was and what might have been
are as if they never were, but the wind's
the same wind and the chair's the same chair for
    remembering and judging
and the plowman in the picture goes on plowing
what has always been, and sowing
what will never be.

[CB / CK]

9

A Tall Girl and Very Precise

A tall girl with butterfly kisses
of a little child,
with earrings
to reinforce her 'yes' and her 'no'.
A silver mezuzah cameo round her neck –
but a mezuzah brings luck only to a door.

A tall girl and very precise,
like a bell tower,
from the top down
a bell at each floor –
like the tower at Attoor
on the Mount of Olives.

She too is preparing herself
to become a beautiful landscape –
a color postcard, without me,
with the sun from behind.

[YA / TH]

A Weeping Mouth

A weeping mouth and a laughing mouth
in terrible battle before a silent crowd.

Each gets hold of the mouth, tears and bites
the mouth, smashes it to shreds and bitter blood.

Till the weeping mouth surrenders and laughs,
till the laughing mouth surrenders and weeps.

[YA / TH]

The Voyeur

A woman dealing with matters of the past
Is in bed with a man who does things of the present.
A sorceress and an owner of modern vehicles.

Her white dress hangs on a string on the porch
And cools the hot night.
Next to her, his colorful shirt, sleeves drooping,
Still dripping, praying upside down.

Together, they exercise a long lovemaking
As reparation for everything.
All their forefathers dreamed of doing
They do to each other,
A lot from behind, a lot like animals.

At midnight, comes the bearded voyeur,
Peeps through the shutters,
Perhaps he's one of the latest prophets
Collecting material for his visions.

[BH / BH]

A Young Girl Goes Out in the Morning,
Like a Knight

A young girl goes out in the morning
Pony-tailed and swaying as if on horseback.

Dresses and handbags, sunglasses, chain and buckles,
Are like armor on her.
But beneath all this
She's light and slender.

Sometimes at night she's naked and alone.
And sometimes she's naked and not alone.

You can hear the sound of bare feet
Running away: that was death.

And afterwards the sound of a kiss
Like the fluttering of a moth
Caught between two panes of glass.

[GA / TP]

Above the Gate of the Hotel

Above the gate of the hotel, I saw a sign:
'International Conference on Inflammations of the Eye'
of those who have cried too much or not cried enough.
All of them with name tags on their lapels
like the temporary markers in a cemetery or the tags in a
   botanical garden.
They approach one another as if sniffing, as if checking,
who are you where are you from and when
was the last time you cried.
The subject of the morning session is Sobbing:
The end of Crying or the Way It Begins. Sobbing
as soul-stuttering and griefstones: Sobbing
as a valve or a loop that links cry to cry,
a loop that opens easily, like a hair ribbon,
and the crying – hair that fans out in profusion, glorious.
Or a loop that turns into an impossible knot,
sobbing like an oath, a testimony, a cure.
And the translators, all women, sit in their cubicles
   translating
fate to fate, cry to cry. And at night they return home,

wash the words off themselves, and love
with sobbings of happiness, their joyous eyes aflame.

[CB / CK]

Advanced Training for Angels

After the training on round targets
(my life is round like them,
with the black bull's-eye of my childhood
in the center, where I'm vulnerable),
after the training on round targets,
training with dummy men: a head
like a head. A man fleeing.
Or people passing slowly:
a child playing, a man seated in his chair,
my love, at her window,
all passing slowly before the riflemen
on the hill of the broken red
tiles at the edge of the world.

[HS]

A Dog after Love

After you left me
I let a dog smell at
My chest and my belly. It will fill its nose
And set out to find you.

I hope it will tear the
Testicles of your lover and bite off his penis

Or at least
Will bring me your stockings between his teeth.

[YA / TH]

Resurrection

Afterward they will get up
all together, and with a sound of chairs scraping
they will face the narrow exit.

And their clothes are crumpled
and covered with dust and cigarette ashes
and their hand discovers in the inside pocket
a ticket stub from a very previous season.

And their faces are still crisscrossed
with God's will.
And their eyes are red from so much sleeplessness
under the ground.

And right away, questions:
What time is it?
Where did you put mine?
When? When?

And one of them can be seen in an ancient
scanning of the sky, to see if rain.
Or a woman,
with an age-old gesture, wipes her eyes
and lifts the heavy hair
at the back of her neck.

[SM]

White Negress

Again I long for
strange, lighted windows;
Maybe a man, maybe stands, maybe
before a mirror.
Or that white snow falls inside.
A strange king lies
on a woman that might have
been mine.

A white negress on the Street of the Abyssinians
that has the voice of a daring boy
before it breaks.

When I'll sit with her in a hot bath
I'll hear from the alleys
arguments on religions.

[HS]

All the Generations Before Me

All the generations before me
donated me, bit by bit, so that I'd be
erected all at once
here in Jerusalem, like a house of prayer
or a charitable institution.
It binds. My name's
my donors' name.
It binds.

I'm approaching the age
of my father's death. My last
will's patched with many patches.

I have to change my life and death
daily to fulfil all the prophecies
prophesied for me. So they're not lies.
It binds.

I've passed forty.
There are jobs I cannot get
because of this. Were I in Auschwitz
they would not have sent me out to work,
but gassed me straightaway.
It binds.

   [HS]

My Parents' Migration

And my parent's migration has not yet calmed in me.
My blood goes on shaking at its walls.
As the bowl after it is set down.
And my parents' migration has not yet calmed in me.
Winds continually over stones.
Earth forgets the footsteps of those who walk.
An awful fate. Stumps of talk after midnight.
An achievement, a retreat. Night reminds
And day forgets.
My eyes which have looked a long time into a vast desert,
Are a little calmed. One woman. The rules of a game
Nobody had ever completely explained. The laws of pain
   and weight.

Even now my heart
Makes only a bare living
With its daily love.
My parents in their migration.

On the crossroads where I am forever orphaned,
Too young to die, too old to play.
The weariness of the miner
The emptiness of the quarry
In one body.
Archaeology of the future
Museums of what is still to happen.
And my parents' migration has not yet calmed in me,
And from bitter peoples I learned bitter languages
For my silence among the houses
Which are always
Like ships.

Already my veins, my tendons
Are a tangle of ropes I will never undo
Finally, my own
Death
And an end to my parents' migration.

[AG / TH]

And There Are Days

And there are days when everyone says, I was there,
I'm ready to testify, I stood a short distance away from
    the accident,
from the bomb, the crucifixion, I almost got hit, almost
    got crucified.
I saw the faces of bride and groom under the *chuppah* and
    almost rejoiced.
When David lay with Bathsheba I was the voyeur,
I happened to be there on the roof fixing the pipes, taking
    down a flag.

With my own eyes I saw the Chanukah miracle in the
    Temple,
I saw General Allenby entering Jaffa Gate,
I saw God.
And then there are days when everything's an alibi:
    wasn't there didn't hear
I heard the explosion only from a distance and I split, saw
    the smoke but
was reading a newspaper. I was staying in some other
    place.
I didn't see God, I've got witnesses.
And the God of Jerusalem is the eternal alibi God,
wasn't there didn't see didn't hear
was in some other place. Was some Place, some Other.

[CB / CK]

chuppah: the wedding canopy. Place (Heb. *Makom*) is one of the
names of God.

As for the World

As for the world,
I am always like one of Socrates' disciples,
Walking by his side,
Hearing his opinions and histories
It remains for me to say:
Yes. Yes it is like that.
You are right again,
Indeed your words are true.

As for my life,
I am always like Venice:
Whatever is mere streets in others
Within me is a dark streaming love.

As for the cry, as for the silence,
I am always a *Shofar*:
All year hoarding its one blast
For the Terrible Days.

As for action
I am always like Cain:
Nomad
In the face of the act, which I will not do,
Or, having done,
Will make it irredeemable.

As for the palm of your hand,
As for the signals of my heart,
And the plans of my flesh,
As for the writing on the wall,
I am always ignorant,
I can neither read nor write
And my head is like the

Heads of those senseless weeds

Knowing only the rustle and drift
Of the wind
When a fate passes through me
To some other place.

[AG / TH]

Beautiful are the Families in Jerusalem

Beautiful are the families in Jerusalem:
A mother from a Russian curse, a father from a Spanish
    curse,
A sister from an Arab curse and brothers from a Torah
    curse
Sitting together on the balcony
On a summer's day in the scent of jasmine.

Beautiful are the houses in Jerusalem:
They are all mines on fixed fuses and therefore
There's no need to worry when you step on a threshold,
Turn the knob or shake hands.
If the time hasn't come there's no danger.

Yes,
Mr Detonator,
Mrs Coil,
Wick boy,
Fuse girl,
Timing device lads,
Always sensitive, so sensitive.

   [GA / TP]

The Last Word

Because my head hasn't grown
since I stopped growing, and my memories
have piled up inside me,
I have to assume they're now in my belly
and my thighs and legs. A sort of walking archive, an
    orderly

disorder, a sagging warehouse, an over-
loaded ship.

Sometimes I want to lie down on a park bench:
that would change my status
from Lost Inside to
Lost Outside.

Words have begun to abandon me
as rats abandon a sinking ship.
The last word is the captain.

[CB]

Dennis was Very Sick

Dennis was very sick.
His face retreated
But his eyes advanced from it
With great courage.
As in a war
When the fresh reinforcements
Pass on their way to the front
The retreating columns of the beaten.

He has to get healthy soon.
He is like our bank,
In which we deposited all we had in our heart.
He is like Switzerland,
Filled with banks.

Already he is smoking one cigarette,
Trembling a little,
And as it should be with a true poet,

He puts the burned matches
Back into the box.

Instructions for a Waitress

Don't remove the glasses and plates
from the table. Don't rub
the stain from the cloth. It's good to know:
people were here before me.

I buy shoes which were on another man's feet.
(My friend has thoughts of his own.)
My love is another man's wife.
My night is 'used' with dreams.
On my window raindrops are painted,
in the margins of my books are notes by others.
On the plan of the house in which I want to live
the architect has drawn strangers near the entrance.
On my bed is a pillow, with
a hollow of a head now gone.

During Our Love Houses were Completed

During our love houses were completed
And someone, beginning then,
Learned to play the flute. His études
Rise and fall. You can hear them
Now when we no longer fill each other
As birds fill a tree,

And you change coins, compulsively,
From country to country,
From urge to urge.

And even though we acted madly,
Now it seems we didn't swerve much
From the norm, didn't disturb
The world, its people and their sleep.
But now it's over.

Soon
Of us two there won't be left either
To forget the other.

   [HS]

The Sweet Breakdowns of Abigail

Everyone whacks her with tiny blows
the way you peel an egg.

With desperate bursts of perfume
she strikes back at the world.

With sharp giggles she gets even
for all the sadness,

and with quick little fallings-in-love,
like burps and hiccups of feeling.

A terrorist of sweetness,
she stuffs bombshells with despair and cinnamon,
with cloves, with shrapnel of love,

23

At night when she tears off her jewelry,
there's a danger she won't know when to stop
and will go on tearing and slashing away at her whole life.

[CB]

from The Visit of the Queen of Sheba

4 *The Voyage Through the Red Sea*

Fish exhaled through the water,
through the long wait. Skippers
navigated by her yearnings' map, by
her belly's rings. Her nipples
accosted her like undercover men.
Her hairs exchanged whispers like conspirators.
In dark corners between sea and dolphin
the counting was quietly begun.
A solitary bird chirped amidst
the constant warbling of her blood. Rules
dropped out of textbooks. Clouds were
ripped to shreds like treaties. At noon
she dreamt about intercourse in the white snow,
about yolk and the pleasures of yellow wax.
The air rushed to enter her lungs. The mariners
babbled in piscatory gobbledygook.

But under the world, under the sea
cantillation reigned supreme:
everyone chanted everyone.

5 *King Solomon is Waiting*

Never any rain,
never a drop of rain.

Always a nebulous fixture,
always a husky love.

The wild-goose-chasers
were back from the pasture.
In the courts of the world
stone-flowers blossomed,
dedicated to alien gods.
Trembling ladders dreamt
about those who were
dreaming about them.

Yet he saw
the world's lining
torn slightly open.
Yet he was wakeful
like so many stables
in Meggido.

Never a drop of rain,
never a drop of rain.
Always a husky love.
Always a quarry.

7 The Duel of Riddles

In the ping-pong of questions and answers
no sound was heard
save PING-PONG,
the counsellors' cough,
sharp tearing of paper.
He made black billows in his beard
to drown her speech.
She turned her hair into a jungle
that he should stray in it.

Words were set down with a clang
like chessmen.
Tall-masted thoughts
overreached one another.
Empty jigsaws filled out
like stellar vacuities.
Secret hoards were exhumed,
buckles and vows undone.
Ruthless religions
were tickled
and laughed horribly.

Her tongue fell over his
in the final game.
Maps were pinpointed on the table.
Everything was open, poignant,
pitiless.

8 *The Empty Hall*

No word-games
were returned to their boxes.
No box was shut
when the game was over.

Sawdust of quizzes,
nutshells of parables,
woolly stuffing for
delicate riddles.

Coarse burlap for
love and contrivance.
Cast-off conundrums
rustling in the litter.

Long-winded problems
wound on a spool,
miracles thrust into cages,
chess-knights forced back into stalls.

Empty crates
(*'Handle with care'*) –
empty crates
sang hymns and anthems.

Then the Kings Guards marched upon her
and she fled, dejected,
like a swarthy snake
in the withered grass.

An indulgent moon circled the towers
as it did on the Eve of Atonement.
Caravans set out unmanned, uncamelled
went voicelessly on and on and on.

[AB]

Return from Ein Gedi

From the green and hidden lushness of Ein Gedi
We returned to the hard city. I called you Rejah
After the Arab name of the wadi
And after the Hebrew word for yearning.
We came back to our empty room already let to others.
On the floor a torn mattress and orange peels
And a sock, a newspaper and other knives for the heart.

What did we learn at Ein Gedi? To make love in the water;
What else? That the mountains are more beautiful as
    they crumble.

Once more we looked out of the arched window
Together we saw the same valley, but each of us
Saw a different future, like two fortune-tellers
Who disagree with each other in a serious and silent
    encounter.

A day after we left thousands of years had already passed.
The piece of paper on which was written 'Same place
Tomorrow at seven' had yellowed and crumpled straight
    away
Like the face of a child born old.

[GA / TP]

The Death of A.G.

Half an hour ago
my crying stopped.
It's strange and quiet now,
like a factory at evening.

I want to make propaganda
for your death.
I sift your letters
from the others
set apart for life – not so long,
and maybe not better.
I pull the sky down close to my eyes
like someone nearsighted,
to read.

I can't understand your death in London
in the mist,

as I can't understand
my life, here in the bright light.

[HS]

How Did a Flag

How did a flag come into being?
Let's assume that in the beginning
there was something whole, which was
then torn into two pieces, both big enough
for two battling armies.

Or like the ragged striped fabric
of a beach chair in an abandoned
little garden of my childhood,
flapping in the wind. This
too could be a flag making you arise
to follow it or to weep at its side,
to betray it or to forget.

I don't know. In my wars
no flag-bearer marched in front
of the gray soldiers in clouds of dust and smoke.
I've seen things starting as spring,
ending up with hasty retreat
in pale dunes.
I'm far away from all that, like one
who in the middle of a bridge
forgets both its ends
and remains standing there
bent over the railing

to look down into the streaming water:
This too is a flag.

[YA / TH]

Human Bodies

Human bodies are different from each other
But their souls are alike, full of brilliant utility,
Like airports.
Do not give me your soul,
Give me your body which I shall never know to the full,
Give me the vessel and not its contents.

Stand with me in airports
Where the pain of parting is dressed up
In pretty words, like orphans,
Where drinks and food are expensive
But people and their destinies cheap.

A man talks into a telephone
And his mouth drinks sorrow and love from the receiver.

Even those who cry have
Hands white as brides,
Arms free from embracing,
What will they do in the world?

Let my soul die with my body.

[BH / BH]

I am Big and Fat

I am big and fat.
Against every ounce of fat
was added an ounce of sadness.

I was a great stutterer, but since
I learned to lie, my speech pours out like water.
Only my face stayed heavy,
like syllables impossible to pronounce,
stumble-stones, stammering.

Sometimes my eyes still show flashes
like fire from remote guns
very far inside me. Old battle.

I demand of others
not to forget. Myself, only to forget.

In the end, forgotten.

[HS]

A Memory Advancing into the Future

I am standing now in the landscape
Which we both looked at from the hillock:
Trees swaying in the wind
Like people swaying at the Apocalypse.

The happiness of their near distance
Was unbearable. We said what a
Pity we don't have more time. 'If we
Come here next time, we'll go there.'

I'm there.
I have time enough.
I'm the next time.

[YA / TH]

The Force of Things Past

I ask myself at what speed the force of things past
reaches me. With the velocity of melting snows
that flows from Mount Hermon all the way down to the
   Dead Sea
or a heavy slow stream of lava from an erupting volcano
or stalactites dripping in a cavern.
I do not know. On my desk there's a broken stone
with AMEN carved on it, a stone from a Jewish grave of a
   thousand years ago.
Now it's on my desk weighting down papers so they
   won't fly away,
and there it is: an ornament, a toy of history and fate.
Also on my desk there's a fragment of a hand grenade
that didn't kill me and there it is, free as a butterfly.

[CB / CK]

Tel Garth

I brought my children to the mound
Where once I fought battles,
So they would understand the things I did do
And forgive me for the things I didn't do.

The distance between my striding legs and my head
Grows bigger and I grow smaller.
Those days grow away from me,
These times grow away from me too,
And I'm in the middle, without them, on this mound
With my children.

A light afternoon wind blows
But only a few people move in the blowing wind,
Bend down a little with the grass and the flowers.
Dandelions cover the mound.
You could say, as dandelions in multitude.

I brought my children to the mound
And we sat there, 'on its back and its side'
As in the poem by Shmuel Ha-Nagid in Spain,
Like me, a man of hills and a man of wars,
Who sang a lullaby to his soldiers before the battle.

Yet I did not talk to my heart, as he did,
But to my children. To the mound, we were the
    resurrection,
Fleeting like this springtime, eternal like it too.

[BH / BH]

I Dreamed a Dream

I dreamed a dream: in my dream seven maidens
fat and sleek came up to the meadow
and I made love to them in the meadow.
And seven skinny windscorched maidens came up after
    them
and swallowed up the fat ones with their hungry thighs,

but their stomachs remained flat.
I made love to them too and they swallowed me too.

But she who solved the dream for me,
the one I really loved,
was both fat and thin,
both swallower and swallowed.

And the day after her I knew
that I would never return to that place.

And the spring after her, they changed the flowers in the
    field
and the telephone books with all their names.

And in the years after her, war broke out
and I knew I would dream no more.

[GA / TP]

Since Then

I fell in battle at Ashdod
In the War of Independence.
My mother said then, he's twenty-four,
And she lights a candle of remembrance
Like birthday candles
You blow out on a cake.

Since then my father died of pain and sorrow
Since then my sisters married
And named their children after me,
Since then my house is my grave and my grave, my
    house,
For I fell in the pale sands
Of Ashdod.

Since then all the cypresses and all the orange trees
Between Negbah and Yad Mordechai
Walk in a slow funeral procession,
Since then all my children and all my fathers
Are orphaned and bereaved
Since then all my children and all my fathers
Walk together with linked hands
In a demonstration against death.
For I fell in the war
In the soft sands of Ashdod.

I carried my comrade on my back.
Since then I always feel his dead body
Like a weighted heaven upon me,
Since then he feels my arched back under him,
Like an arched segment of the earth's crust.
For I fell in the terrible sands of Ashdod
Not just him.

And since then I compensate myself for my death
With loves and dark feasts
Since then I am of blessed memory,
Since then I don't want God to avenge me.
Since then I don't want my mother to cry for me
With her handsome, precise face,
Since then I battle against pain,
Since then I march against my memories
Like a man against the wind,
Since then I weep for my memories
Like a man for his dead,
Since then I put out my memories
Like a man, a fire.
Since then I am silent.

For I fell at Ashdod
In the War of Independence.

'Emotions erupted!' so they said then, 'Hopes
Mounted,' so they said but say no more,
'The arts burgeoned,' so said the history books,
'Science flourished,' so they said then,
'The evening breeze cooled
Their burning brow,' so they said then,
'The morning breeze ruffled their hair,'
So they said.
But since then winds do other things
And since then words say other things
(Don't tell me I'm alive),
For I fell in the soft, pale sands
Of Ashdod in the War of Independence.

[GA / TP]

Love Gifts

I gave you, for
your earlobes, for your fingers,
I gilded the time on your wrist,
I hung many shining things on you
so that you'd move in the wind
for me, chime softly over my head,
to soothe my sleep.

I stuffed your bed with apples
(as it is written in the Song of Songs)
so we'd roll smoothly
on a red, apple-bearing bed.

I covered your skin with delicate pink fabric
transparent as baby lizards
which have eyes of black diamonds in summer nights.

You enabled me to live for a few months
without needing a religion
or a *Weltanschauung.*

You gave me a letter opener of silver:
letters like these aren't opened like that. They're
torn open, torn, torn.

[HS]

Half-sized Violin

I sat in the playground where I played as a child.
The child went on playing in the sand. His hands went on
making *pat-pat*, then dig then destroy,
then *pat-pat* again.

Between the trees that little house is still standing
where the high-voltage hums and threatens.
On the iron door a skull-and-crossbones: another
old childhood acquaintance.

When I was nine they gave me
a half-sized violin and half-sized feelings.

Sometimes I'm still overcome by pride
and a great joy: I already know
how to dress and undress
all by myself.

[CB]

Savage Memories

I think these days of the wind in your hair,
and of my years in the world which preceded your
    coming,
and of the eternity to which I proceed before you;

and I think of the bullets that did not kill me,
but killed my friends –
they who were better than me because
they did not go on living;

and I think of you standing in summer
naked before the stove,
or bending, the better to read it, over a book
in the last light of day.

Yes, we had more than life.
We must now balance everything
with heavy dreams, and set
savage memories
upon what was once today.

   [RF]

I Walked past a House Where I Lived Once

I walked past a house where I lived once:
a man and a woman are still together in the whispers
    there.
Many years have passed with the quiet hum
of the staircase bulb going on
and off and on again.

The keyholes are like little wounds
where all the blood seeped out. And inside,
people as pale as death.

I want to stand once again as I did
holding my first love all night long in the doorway.
When we left at dawn, the house
began to fall apart and since then the city and since then
the whole world.

I want to be filled with longing again
till dark burn marks show on my skin.

I want to be written again
in the Book of Life, to be written every single day
till the writing hand hurts.

[CB]

I Wasn't One of the Six Million

I wasn't one of the six million
who died in the Shoah, I wasn't even among the survivors,
and I wasn't one of the six hundred thousand who went
    out of Egypt
I arrived at the promised land by sea,
no, I wasn't in that number, though I still have the fire
    and the smoke
inside me, the pillars of fire and the pillars of smoke
    guide me
by night and by day, I still have inside me the crazy
    search
for emergency exits for soft places
for the nakedness of the land for the escape into weakness
and hope, I still have inside me the lust to search

for living water with quiet talk to the rock and with
    crazed smitings.
Afterwards, silence: no questions, no answers.
Jewish history and world history
grind me between them like two grindstones, sometimes
to a powder, and the solar year and the lunar year
get ahead of each other or fall behind,
they leap and set my life in perpetual motion.
Sometimes I fall into the gap between them to hide out
or to sink down.

[CB/CK]

On My Return

I will not be greeted on my return
by children's voices, or by the barking
of a loyal dog, or by blue smoke rising
as it happens in legends.

There won't happen for me any 'and he
lifted his eyes' – as
in the Bible – 'and behold.'

I have crossed the border of being an orphan.
It's a long time since they called me
an ex-serviceman.
I'm not protected anymore.

But I have invented the dry weeping.
And who has invented this
has invented the beginning of the world's end,
the crack and the tumbling down and the end.

[YA/TH]

40

I Feel Good in My Trousers

If the Romans hadn't glorified their victory
With the Arch of Titus, we wouldn't know
The shape of the Menorah from the Temple.
But we know the shape of Jews
Because they multiplied unto me.

I feel good in my trousers
In which my victory is hidden
Even though I know I'll die
And even though I know the Messiah won't come,
I feel good.

I'm made from remnants of flesh and blood
And leftovers of philosophies. I'm the generation
Of the pot-bottom: sometimes at night
When I can't sleep,
I hear the hard spoon scratching
And scraping the bottom of the pot.

But I feel good in my trousers,
I feel good.

[GA / TP]

In Rabbi Kook Street

I'm going up Rabbi Kook Street
without this good man.
A religious hat he wore for prayer
silk cylinder for government
fly in the wind of the dead
over me, float on the face of the water
of my dreams.

I get to Prophets Street, there aren't any,
and the Street of the Ethiopians, there are several. I'm
scouting out where you'll live after me,
I weave the nest for you alone,
fix my pain's place with my brow's sweat,
check the road you'll get back by
and the windows of your room, big wound,
between shut and open, light and dark.

Cake smells from inside the ruin,
a shop where they give out Bibles free,
free, free. More than one prophet's
emerged from this tangle of alleys
as if all's caved in and he becomes another.

I'm going up Rabbi Kook Street,
on your back your bed like a cross,
though it's hard to suppose
a woman's bed the icon of a new religion.

[DS]

A Quiet Joy

I'm standing in a place where I once loved.
The rain is falling. The rain is my home.

I think words of longing: a landscape
out to the very edge of what's possible.

I remember you waving your hand
as if wiping mist from the windowpane,

and your face, as if enlarged
from an old blurred photo.

Once I committed a terrible wrong
to myself and others.

But the world is beautifully made for doing good
and for resting, like a park bench

And late in life I discovered
a quiet joy
like a serious disease that's discovered too late:

just a little time left now for quiet joy.

[CB]

A Czech Refugee in London

In a very short black velvet skirt,
A refugee of policies. (Her father in prison there.)
Her cunt very powerful, like the only eye
Of a war hero.
With her white thighs she walks strongly
Under this gray sky. 'Each one in his time
Does his duty.' With us it's
Many deserts with caves and holes to hide:
'Does the things he has to do.'

She behaves here as in a schoolbook for foreign languages:
In the morning she gets up. She washes. (She
Doesn't think about me.) She dresses.
She comes back in the evening. She reads.
(She'll never think about me.) She sleeps.

'At the end of spring, when the air softens,
I find out every year that I'm without defenses.'

[YA / TH]

43

Not Far from Death

In Latrun, not far from the death on the hill
And the silence in the buildings, stands a woman
On the side of the road. Next to her, a shiny new car,
Motor gaping in amazement, waiting
To be towed to a safe place.
The woman is beautiful. Her face, confidence and rage.
Her dress a love banner. A very passionate woman,
Inside her stands her dead father
Like a quiet soul. I knew him alive,
I greeted him when I passed by.

[BH / BH]

Latrun: a Trappist monastery and the site of a fierce battle in the
Israeli War of Independence.

In My Worst Dreams

In my worst dreams
You, with bright eyes,
Are always standing near walls
Whose foundation stone
Is a heart.

Of all the things I do.
Parting is the inevitable one.

In my dreams I always hear a voice –
It is not my voice –
And not yours,
Neither is it the daughter of your voice.

Eyes creased, my eyes are
Like the eyes of exhausted beasts
Lusting for days
That have passed with the nights.

They have taken a love-mask off me
Just as they take a death-mask.
They took it without my noticing
As I lay beside you.

It is my true face.

[AG / TH]

In the Middle of Summer Suddenly a Smell of Rain

In the middle of summer suddenly a smell of rain:
A memory of what was and a prophecy of what will be.
But the middle of summer is empty.

As when you find a lost child
After a long search and the joy
Of finding him cancels the anger
And the rising anger destroys the joy,

Or like the sound of a slammed door
Some time after people have left,

Or like a man who holds out a woman's photograph to be
    punched
Instead of a ticket.
And he's let through.

[AG]

In the Middle of this Century

In the middle of this century we turned to each other
With half faces and full eyes
Like an ancient Egyptian picture
And for a short while.

I stroked your hair
In the opposite direction to your journey,
We called to each other,
Like calling out the names of towns
Where nobody stops
Along the route.

Lovely is the world rising early to evil,
Lovely is the world falling asleep to sin and pity,
In the mingling of ourselves, you and I,
Lovely is the world.

The earth drinks men and their loves
Like wine,
To forget.
It can't.
And like the contours of the Judean hills,
We shall never find peace.

In the middle of this century we turned to each other,
I saw your body, throwing shade, waiting for me,
The leather straps for a long journey
Already tightening across my chest.
I spoke in praise of your mortal hips,
You spoke in praise of my passing face,
I stroked your hair in the direction of your journey,
I touched your flesh, prophet of your end,

I touched your hand which has never slept,
I touched your mouth which may yet sing.

Dust from the desert covered the table
At which we did not eat.
But with my finger I wrote on it
The letters of your name.

[AG]

In the Morning It was Still Night

In the morning it was still night and the lights were on
when we rose from happiness like people
who rise from the dead,
and like them in an instant each of us remembered
a former life. That's why we separated.

You put on an old-fashioned blouse of striped silk
and a tight skirt, a stewardess of goodbyes
from some earlier generation,
and already our voices were like loudspeakers,
announcing times and places.

From your leather bag with its soft folds, like an old
    woman's cheeks,
you took out lipstick, a passport, and a letter sharp-edged
    as a knife,
and put them on the table.
Then you put everything away again.

I said, I'll move back a little, as at an exhibition,
to see the whole picture. And
I haven't stopped moving back.

Time is as light as froth,
the heavy sediment stays in us forever.

[CB]

Gevaram

In these low hills, a life
that was meant to be a long one came to its end,
and what we thought was smoke
proved more steady than our passing lives.
Even the abandoned derricks became a part
of this good landscape, signposts for places of love and
    death
like the trees and the water towers.

This winter the river tore whole chunks out of the
    almond grove.
The roots of the trees were exposed,
beautiful as branches in the sunlight,
but for a few days only.

Here the sand dunes hand themselves down to the
    limestone
and the limestone to the light soil, and the light
to the heavy, and the heavy to the boulders
at the edge of the coastal plain. Handing-down and
    continuity,
tradition and change without human beings,
abundance and sinking. And the droning of the bees
is the droning of time.

In Gevaram, in a wooden shack, I once saw
books by Buber and Rilke on the shelf

and prints of Van Gogh and Modigliani.
It was the night before a deadly battle.

And there's a grove of eucalyptus trees,
pale, as if sick with longing.
They don't know what they're longing for
and I tell them now in a quiet voice:
Australia, Australia.

[CB]

from Anniversaries of War

Huleikat – The Third Poem about Dicky

In these hills, even the towers of oil wells
Are a mere memory. Here Dicky fell,
Four years older than me, like a father to me
In times of trouble and distress. Now I am older than him
By forty years and I remember him
Like a young son, and I am his father, old and grieving.

And you, who remember only faces,
Do not forget the hands stretched out,
The feet running lightly,
The words.
Remember: even the departure to terrible battles
Passes by gardens and windows
And children playing, a dog barking.

Remind the fallen fruit
Of its leaves and branches,
Remind the sharp thorns
How soft and green they were in springtime,
And do not forget,

Even a fist
Was once an open palm and fingers.

The Shore of Ashkelon

Here, at the shore of Ashkelon, we reached the end of
    memory,
Like rivers reaching the sea.
The near past sinks into the far past,
And from the depths, the far overflows the near.
Peace to him that is far off and to him that is near.

Here, among the broken statues and pillars,
I ask how did Samson bring down the temple
Standing eyeless, saying: 'Let me die with the
    Philistines.'

Did he embrace the pillars as in a last love
Or did he push them away with his arms,
To be alone in his death.

What Did I Learn in the Wars

What did I learn in the wars:
To march in time to swinging arms and legs
Like pumps pumping an empty well.

To march in a row and be alone in the middle,
To dig into pillows, featherbeds, the body of a beloved
    woman,
And to yell 'Mama', when she cannot hear,
And to yell 'God', when I don't believe in Him,
And even if I did believe in Him
I wouldn't have told Him about the war
As you don't tell a child about grown-ups' horrors.

What else did I learn. I learned to reserve a path for
    retreat.
In foreign lands I rent a room in a hotel
Near the airport or railroad station.
And even in wedding halls
Always to watch the little door
With the 'Exit' sign in red letters.

A battle too begins
Like rhythmical drums for dancing and ends
With a 'retreat at dawn'. Forbidden love
And battle, the two of them sometimes end like this.

But above all I learned the wisdom of camouflage,
Not to stand out, not to be recognized,
Not to be apart from what's around me,
Even not from my beloved.
Let them think I am a bush or a lamb,
A tree, a shadow of a tree,
A doubt, a shadow of a doubt,
A living hedge, a dead stone,
A house, a corner of a house.

If I were a prophet I would have dimmed the glow of the
    vision
And darkened my faith with black paper
And covered the magic with nets.

And when my time comes, I shall don the camouflage
    garb of my end:
The white clouds and a lot of sky blue
And stars that have no end.

[BH / BH]

Into an Excavation

Into an abandoned excavation
There fell a small toy,
And while the child was still weeping
And the sound of his lament
Was reaching into the rest of his life, a thistledown
Prepared to hover over the dry lands.

And an ageing teacher, who waited many years
For a girl to grow up
Is lying with her now, his mouth gaping like the dead.

An hour turned into a knife
To be used only once.

'Life will wipe that smile off your face,'
So they warned. 'Time will wipe the tears
From your eyes,' so they promised.
There will be many smiles left on time
There will be many tears smeared on life
Like on a good towel.

[GA / TP]

Love Song

It started like this: In the heart it became
loose and easy and happy, as
when someone feels his bootlaces loosening a bit
and bends down.

After this came other days.

Now I'm like a Trojan Horse
filled with terrible loves:
Each night they break out and run amok
and at dawn they come back
into my dark belly.

[YA / TH]

Mayor

It's sad
To be the Mayor of Jerusalem.
It is terrible.
How can any man be the mayor of a city like that?

What can he do with her?
He will build, and build, and build.

And at night
The stones of the hills round about
Will crawl down
Towards the stone houses,
Like wolves coming
To howl at the dogs
Who have become men's slaves.

[AG / TH]

I've Filtered out of the Book of Esther

I've filtered out of the Book of Esther the residue
of vulgar joy, and out of the Book of Jeremiah
the howl of pain in the guts. And out of the
Song of Songs the endless search for love,

53

and out of the Book of Genesis the dreams
and Cain, and out of Ecclesiastes
the despair and out of the Book of Job – Job.
And from what was left over I pasted for myself a new
    Bible.
Now I live censored and pasted and limited and in peace.

A woman asked me last night in the darkened street
about the well-being of another woman
who had died before her time, and not in anyone's time.
Out of great tiredness I answered her:
She's fine, she's fine.

[YA / TH]

Jerusalem is Full of Used Jews

Jerusalem is full of used Jews, worn out by history,
Jews secondhand, slightly damaged, at bargain prices.
And the eye yearns toward Zion all the time. And all the
    eyes
of the living and the dead are cracked like eggs
on the rim of the bowl, to make the city
puff up rich and fat.

Jerusalem is full of tired Jews,
always goaded on again for holidays, for memorial days,
like circus bears dancing on aching legs.

What does Jerusalem need? It doesn't need a mayor,
it needs a ringmaster, whip in hand,
who can tame prophecies, train prophets to gallop
around and around in a circle, teach its stones to line up
in a bold, risky formation for the grand finale.

Later they'll jump back down again
to the sound of applause and wars.

And the eye yearns toward Zion, and weeps.

[CB]

Jacob and the Angel

Just before dawn she sighed and held him
that way, and defeated him.
And he held her that way, and defeated her,
and both of them knew that a hold
brings death.
They agreed to do without names.

But in the first light
he saw her body,
which remained white in the places
the swimsuit covered, yesterday.

Then someone called her suddenly from above,
twice.
The way you call a little girl from playing
in the yard.
And he knew her name; and let her go.

[SM]

To My Mother

I

Like an old windmill
Two hands always raised

To howl at the sky
And two lowered
To make sandwiches.

Her eyes are clean and glitter
Like the Passover eve.

2

At night she will put
All the letters
And the photographs
Side by side.

So she can measure
The length of God's finger.

3

I want to walk in the deep
Wadis between her sobs
I want to stand in the terrible heat
Of her silence.

I want to lean on the
Rough trunks
Of her pain.

4

She laid me,
As Hagar laid Ishmael
Under one of the bushes.

So that she won't have to be at my death
In the war,

Under one of the bushes
In one of the wars.

[AG / TH]

Love is Finished Again

Love is finished again, like a profitable citrus season
or like an archaeological dig that turned up
from deep inside the earth
turbulent things that wanted to be forgotten.

Love is finished again. When a tall building
is torn down and the debris cleared away, you stand there
on the square empty lot, saying: What a small
space that building stood on
with all its many floors and people.

From the distant valleys you can hear
the sounds of a solitary tractor at work
and from the distant past, the sound of a fork
clattering against a porcelain plate,
beating an egg yolk with sugar for a child,
clattering and clattering.

[CB]

Spy

Many years ago
I was sent
To spy out the land
Beyond the age of thirty.

And I stayed there
And didn't go back to my senders,
So as not to be made
To tell
About this land

And made
To lie.

[HS]

Meir Mindlin

Meir Mindlin divorced his name three times,
went back to his first name and left the country. In his
   empty flat
many years ago I loved a great love
because a flat cannot tolerate a void: *horror vacui.*
I don't remember in which war I first met him
and in which history, public or private.
He knew five languages, but when the stroke hit him
he was paralysed and struck dumb in all five tongues.
I want to cleanse his death notice of all the other news on
   the page
the way archaeologists scour a clay pot, or the way
a dead body is cleansed of every impurity.
I want to advertise his life – false advertising
for an item that's gone out of stock, you can't get it
   anymore.
I want rites of mourning, rending clothes,
taking off shoes, lightly, easily, like cursing
because curses are light. It's the blessings that weigh you
   down.

[CB / CK]

Seven Laments for the War-Dead

1

Mr Beringer, whose son
fell at the Canal that strangers dug
so ships could cross the desert,
crosses my path at Jaffa Gate.

He has grown very thin, has lost
the weight of his son.
That's why he floats so lightly in the alleys
and gets caught in my heart like little twigs
that drift away.

2

As a child he would mash his potatoes
to a golden mush.
And then you die.
A living child must be cleaned
when he comes home from playing.
But for a dead man
earth and sand are clear water, in which
his body goes on being bathed and purified forever.

3

The Tomb of the Unknown Soldier
across there. On the enemy's side. A good landmark
for gunners of the future.

Or the war monument in London
at Hyde Park Corner, decorated
like a magnificent cake: yet another soldier
lifting head and rifle,

another cannon, another eagle, another
stone angel.

And the whipped cream of a huge marble flag
poured over it all
with an expert hand.

But the candied, much-too-red cherries
were already gobbled up
by the glutton of hearts. Amen.

4

I came upon an old zoology textbook,
Brehm, Volume II, *Birds*:
in sweet phrases, an account of the life of the starling,
swallow, and thrush. Full of mistakes in an antiquated
Gothic typeface, but full of love, too. 'Our feathered
friends.' 'Migrate from us to the warmer climes.'
Nest, speckled egg, soft plumage, nightingale,
stork. 'The harbingers of spring.' The robin,
red-breasted.

Year of publication: 1913, Germany,
on the eve of the war that was to be
the eve of all my wars.

My good friend who died in my arms, in
his blood,
on the sands of Ashdod. 1948, June

Oh my friend,
red-breasted.

5

Dicky was hit.
Like the water tower at Yad Mordekhai.
Hit. A hole in the belly. Everything
Came flooding out.

But he has remained standing like that
in the landscape of my memory
like the water tower at Yad Mordekhai.

He fell not far from there,
a little to the north, near Houlayqat.

6

Is all of this
sorrow? I don't know.
I stood in the cemetery dressed in
the camouflage clothes of a living man: brown pants
and a shirt yellow as the sun.

Cemeteries are cheap; they don't ask for much.
Even the wastebaskets are small, made for holding
tissue paper
that wrapped flowers from the store.
Cemeteries are a polite and disciplined thing.
'I shall never forget you,' in French
on a little ceramic plaque.
I don't know who it is that won't ever forget:
he's more anonymous than the one who died.

Is all of this sorrow? I guess so.
'May ye find consolation in the building
of the homeland.' But how long
can you go on building the homeland

and not fall behind in the terrible
three-sided race
between consolation and building and death?

Yes, all of this is sorrow. But leave
a little love burning always
like the small bulb in the room of a sleeping baby
that gives him a bit of security and quiet love
though he doesn't know what the light is
or where it comes from.

7

Memorial Day for the war-dead: go tack on
the grief of all your losses –
including a woman who left you –
to the grief of losing them; go mix
one sorrow with another, like history,
that in its economical way
heaps pain and feast and sacrifice
onto a single day for easy reference.

Oh sweet world, soaked like bread
in sweet milk for the terrible
toothless God. 'Behind all this,
some great happiness is hiding.' No use
crying inside and screaming outside.
Behind all this, some great happiness may
be hiding.

Memorial day. Bitter salt, dressed up as
a little girl with flowers.
Ropes are strung out the whole length of the route
for a joint parade: the living and the dead together.

Children move with the footsteps of someone else's grief
as if picking their way through broken glass.

The flautist's mouth will stay pursed for many days.
A dead soldier swims among the small heads
with the swimming motions of the dead,
with the ancient error the dead have
about the place of the living water.

A flag loses contact with reality and flies away.
A store window decked out with beautiful dresses for
    women
in blue and white. And everything
in three languages: Hebrew, Arabic and Death.

A great royal beast has been dying all night long
under the jasmine,
with a fixed stare at the world.
A man whose son died in the war
walks up the street
like a woman with a dead fetus in her womb.
'Behind all this, some great happiness is hiding.'

  [CB]

Eyes

My eldest son's eyes are like black figs
For he was born at the end of the summer.

And my youngest son's eyes are clear
Like orange slices, for he was born in their season.

And the eyes of my little daughter are round
Like the first grapes.

And all are sweet in my worry.

And the eyes of the Lord roam the earth
And my eyes are always looking round my house

God's in the eye business and the fruit business
I'm in the worry business.

[GA / TP]

My Ex-pupil has Become a Policewoman

My ex-pupil has become a policewoman.
There she is, standing at the crossroads in town:
She opens a box made of metal,
like a box of perfumes and cosmetics,
and changes the colors of the traffic lights
according to her mood.

Her eyes are a mixture of green, red and yellow.
her hair is cut very short, like that of fresh street urchins.
In her high black shoes she leans against the box.
Her skirt is short and tight. I don't even dare
to imagine all the terrible glory at the upper
end of all this golden tan.

I don't understand anymore. I'm already lost.
When I walk the street whole legions
of young men and young women are
thrown against me in ever-growing waves.
They seem to have endless reserves.
And my pupil, the policewoman,
is unable to stop them:
She even joins them!

[YA / TH]

My Father Fought Their War for Four Years

My father fought their war for four years
And he didn't hate his enemies or love them.
But I know, that even there
He formed me daily out of his little calms
So rare; he gathered them out of the bombs
And the smoke,
And he put them in his frayed knapsack
With the last bits of his mother's hardening cake.

And with his eyes he gathered nameless dead,
He gathered many dead on my behalf,
So that I will know them in his look and love them.

And not die, like them, in horror . . .

And he filled his eyes with them in vain:

I go out to all my wars.

[AG / TH]

My Father in a White Space Suit

My father, in a white space suit,
walks around with the light, heavy steps of the dead
over the surface of my life that doesn't
hold onto a thing.

He calls out names: This is the Crater of Childhood.
This is an abyss. This happened at your Bar Mitzvah.
   These
are white peaks. This is a deep voice
from then. He takes specimens and puts them away in
   his gear:

65

sand, words, the sighing stones of my dreams.
He surveys and determines. He calls me
the planet of his longings, land of my childhood, his
childhood, our childhood.

'Learn to play the violin, my son. When you are
grown up, music will help you
in difficult moments of loneliness and pain.'
That's what he told me once, but I didn't believe him.

And then he floats, how he floats, into the grief
of his endless white death.

[CB]

Instead of Words

My love has a very long white gown
of sleep, of sleeplessness, of weddings.
In the evening she sits at a small table,
puts a comb down on it, two tiny bottles
and a brush, instead of words.
Out of the depths of her hair she fishes many pins
and puts them in her mouth, instead of words.

I dishevel her, she combs.
I dishevel again. What's left?
She falls asleep instead of words,
and her sleep already knows me,
wags her woolly dreams.
Her belly easily absorbs
all the wrathful prophecies of
the End of Days.

I wake her: we
are the instruments of a hard love.

[CB]

My Mother Once Told Me

My mother once told me
Not to sleep with flowers in the room.
Since then I have not slept with flowers.
I sleep alone, without them.

There were many flowers.
But I've never had enough time.
And persons I love are already pushing themselves
Away from my life, like boats
Away from the shore.

My mother said
Not to sleep with flowers.
You won't sleep.
You won't sleep, mother of my childhood.

The bannister I clung to
When they dragged me off to school
Is long since burnt.
But my hands, clinging,
Remain
Clinging.

[AG / TH]

My Son was Drafted

My son was drafted. We brought him
to the station along with the other boys.
Now his face has joined the faces of those who say
goodbye to me
from the passing windows of the buses and trains of my
life,
faces in the streaming rain, faces
squinting in the sun. And now his face.
In the corner of the window, like a stamp on an envelope.

In a piazza in Rome near the Coliseum I wash my hands
at a public faucet
and drink from my cupped palm, and meanwhile a red-
haired woman
in a white dress who was sitting on a folding chair near a
closed gate
is gone. When I lift my wet face
she is no more, flown away like a feather laid down upon
the world
to check if the world is still breathing. The world
is still breathing, the world is alive
the woman is still alive. We are alive, my son is still alive
the white feather's still flying and living.
I want my son to be a soldier in the Italian army
with a crest of colorful feathers on his cap,
happily dashing around with no enemies, no camouflage.

[CB / CK]

Luxury

My uncle is buried at Sheik Baadar.
The other one is scattered in the Carpathian mountains.

My father is buried in the Synhedria,
My grandmother on the Mount of Olives
And all their forefathers
Are buried in the ruined Jewish cemeteries in the villages
  of Lower Franconia,
Near rivers and forests which are not Jerusalem.

My father's father kept heavy-eyed
Jewish cows in their sheds below the kitchen –

And rose at four in the morning.
I inherited his early rising,
My mouth bitter with nightmares:
I attend to my bad dreams.

Grandfather, Grandfather,
Chief Rabbi of my life,
As you sold unleavened bread on the Passover Eve,
Sell my pains –
So they stay in me, even ache, but not mine,
Not my property.

So many tombstones are scattered behind me –
Names, engraved like the names of long-abandoned
  railway stations.
How shall I cover all these distances,
How can I keep them connected?
I can't afford such an intricate network.
It's a luxury.

[AG / TH]

The Rustle of History's Wings,
as They Said Then

Not far from the railway track beside the painful post
    office
I saw a ceramic plaque on an old house, and I knew
That this was the name of the son of someone whose girl
    I took
Years ago: she left him and came to me
And the young man was born to another woman
And didn't know about all this.

Those were the days of great love and great destiny.
The colonial power imposed a curfew on the city and
    confined us
To sweet love in a room
Guarded by well-armed soldiers.

I paid five shillings and changed my ancestral name
From the diaspora to a proud Hebrew name to match hers.

That whore fled to America, married someone,
A spice broker, pepper, cinnamon and cardamom,
And left me with my new name and the war.

'The rustle of history's wings,' as they said then,
Which almost killed me in battle,
Blew softly over her face.

And with the terrible wisdom of war they told me to
    carry
My first-aid bandage right over my heart
Over the foolish heart that still loved her
And over the wise heart that would forget.

[GA / TP]

70

A Tourist

On a great rock by the Jaffa Gate
sat a golden girl from Scandinavia
and oiled herself with suntan oil
as if on the beach.

I told her, don't go into these alleys,
a net of bachelors in heat is spread there,
a snare of lechers. And further inside,
in half-darkness, the groaning trousers
of old men, and unholy lust in the guise of prayer
and grief and seductive chatter in many languages.

Once Hebrew was God's slang
in these streets,
now I use it for
holy desire.

[GA / TP]

Jerusalem

On a roof in the Old City
laundry hanging in the late afternoon sunlight:
the white sheet of a woman who is my enemy,
the towel of a man who is my enemy,
to wipe off the sweat of his brow.

In the sky of the Old City
a kite.
At the other end of the string,
a child
I can't see
because of the wall.

We have put up many flags,
they have put up many flags.
To make us think that they're happy.
To make them think that we're happy.

[SM]

A Song of Lies on Sabbath Eve

On a Sabbath Eve, at dusk on a summer day
when I was a child
when the odors of food and prayer drifted up from all the
    houses
and the wings of the Sabbath angels rustled in the air,
I began to lie to my father:
'I went to another synagogue.'

I don't know if he believed me or not
but the lie was very sweet in my mouth.
And in all the houses at night
hymns and lies drifted up together,
O taste and see
and in all the houses at night
Sabbath angels died like flies in the lamp,
and lovers put mouth to mouth
and inflated one another till they floated in the air
or burst.

Since then, lying has tasted very sweet to me,
and since then I've always gone to another synagogue.
And my father returned the lie when he died:
'I've gone to another life.'

[CB]

72

The Jewish Time Bomb

On my desk there's a stone with AMEN carved on it, one
   survivor fragment
of the thousands upon thousands of bits of broken
   tombstones
in Jewish graveyards. I know all these broken bits
now fill the great Jewish time bomb
along with the other fragments and shrapnel, broken
   Tablets of the Law
broken altars broken crosses rusty crucifixion nails
broken houseware and holyware and broken bones
eyeglasses shoes prostheses false teeth
and empty tin cans of lethal poison. All these
fill the Jewish time bomb till the End of Days.
And though I know all about these, and all about the End
   of Days,
this stone on my desk gives me peace.
It is the touchstone no one touches, more philosophical
than any philosopher's stone, broken stone from a broken
   tomb
more whole than any wholeness,
a stone of witness to what has always been
and what will always be, a stone of amen and love.
Amen, amen, and may it come to pass.

   [CB / CK]

73

My Father's Memorial Day

On my father's memorial day
I went out to see his mates –
All those buried with him in one row,
His life's graduation class.

I already remember most of their names,
Like a parent collecting his little son
From school, all of his friends.

My father still loves me, and I
Love him always, so I don't weep.
But in order to do justice to this place
I have lit a weeping in my eyes
With the help of a nearby grave –
A child's. 'Our little Yossy, who was
Four when he died.'

[YA / TH]

Letter of Recommendation

On summer nights I sleep naked
in Jerusalem on my bed,
which stands on the brink
of a deep valley
without rolling down into it.

During the day I walk about,
the Ten Commandments on my lips
like an old song someone is humming to himself.

Oh, touch me, touch me, you good woman!
This is not a scar you feel under my shirt.

It's a letter of recommendation, folded,
from my father:
'He is still a good boy and full of love.'

I remember my father waking me up
for early prayers. He did it caressing
my forehead, not tearing the blanket away.

Since then I love him even more.
And because of this
let him be woken up
gently and with love
on the Day of Resurrection.

[YA / TH]

On the Day My Daughter was Born
No One Died

On the day my daughter was born not a single person
died in the hospital, and at the entrance gate
the sign said: 'Today *kohanim* are permitted to enter.'
And it was the longest day of the year.
In my great joy
I drove with my friend to the hills of Sha'ar Ha-Gai.

We saw a bare, sick pine, nothing on it but a lot of pine
cones. Zvi said trees that are about to die produce more
pine cones than healthy trees. And I said to him: That
was a poem and you didn't realise it. Even though you're
a man of the exact sciences, you've made a poem. And he
answered: And you, though you're a man of dream, have
made an exact little girl with all the exact instruments
for her life.

[CB]

Once a Great Love

Once a great love cut my life in two.
The first part goes on twisting
at some other place like a snake cut in two.

The passing years have calmed me
and brought healing to my heart and rest to my eyes.

And I'm like someone standing in
the Judean desert, looking at a sign:
'Sea Level.'
He cannot see the sea, but he knows.

Thus I remember your face everywhere
at your 'face level'.

[YA / TH]

One Sees All Kinds of Things

'One sees all kinds of things,' said the Swedish
officer observing at the armistice line.
'All kinds of things,' and said nothing more.

'One sees a lot of things,' said the old
shoeshine man by the Jaffa gate
when a Swedish girl in a very short dress
stood above him, without looking at him
with her proud eyes.

The prophet who looked into the opening heaven saw,
and so did God, 'all kinds of things' down there beyond
   the smoke,
and the surgeon saw when he cut open a cancerous belly
and closed it again.

'One sees all kinds of things,' said
our ancestor Jacob on his bed after the blessing
which took his last strength. 'All kinds
of things,' and he turned
toward the wall and he died.

[YA / TH]

from Patriotic Songs

I

Our baby was weaned in the first days
of the war. And I ran out to stare
at the terrible desert.

At night I came back again to see him
asleep. Already he's forgetting
his mother's nipples, and he'll go on forgetting
till the next war.

And so, while he was still small,
his hopes were closed, and his complaints
opened wide – never to close again.

2

The war broke out in autumn at the empty border
between sweet grapes and oranges.

The sky is blue, like veins in a woman's tormented
thighs.

The desert is a mirror for those looking at it.

Sad males carry the memory of their families
in carriers and pouches and hunchback-knapsacks
and soul-bags and heavy eye-bladders.

The blood froze in its veins. That's why it can't be
    spilled,
but only broken into pieces.

3

October sun warms our faces.
A soldier is filling bags with soft sand
in which once he played.

October sun warms our dead.
Sorrow is a heavy wooden board.
Tears are nails.

4

I have nothing to say about the war,
nothing to add. I'm ashamed.

All the knowledge I have absorbed in my life
I give up, like a desert
which has given up all water.
Names I never thought I would forget
I'm forgetting.

And because of the war I say again,
for the sake of a last and simple sweetness:
The sun is circling round the earth. Yes.
The earth is flat, like a lost, floating board. Yes.
God is in Heaven. Yes.

5

I've shut myself in. I'm like
a heavy, tight swamp. I sleep war
like hibernation.

They've made me a commander of the dead
on the Mount of Olives.

Always, even in victory,
I lose.

7

The blood erecting the penis
is not semen.

And blood spilled, of course,
is not semen.

And semen drowning in blood is not semen
and blood without semen is nothing
and semen without blood is nil.

8

What has the dead burned man bequeathed to us?
What does the water want us to do?

To make no noise, to keep it clean,
to behave very quietly at its side,
to let it flow.

10

I sometimes think about my fathers
and their forefathers from the destruction
of the temple onward through medieval tortures until me.

I only remember as far back as my grandfather:
He did not have any additional hands,
or a special plug, or a spare navel,
or any instruments to receive and pass on to me.

He was a village Jew, God-fearing
and heavy-eyed. An old man
with a long pipe. My first memory
is of my grandmother with trembling hands
spilling a kettle of boiling water over my feet
when I was two.

11

The town I was born in was destroyed by shells.
The ship in which I sailed to the land of Israel was
    drowned later in the war.

The barn at Hammadia where I had loved was burned
    out.
The sweet shop at Ein-Gedi was blown up by the enemy.
The bridge at Ismailia, which I crossed to and fro on the
    eve of my loves,
has been torn to pieces.

Thus my life is wiped out behind me according to an
    exact map:

How much longer can my memories hold out?

The girl from my childhood was killed and my father is
    dead.

That's why you should never choose me
to be a lover or a son, or a bridge-crosser
or a citizen or a tenant.

15

Even my loves are measured by wars:
I am saying this happened after the Second
World War. We met a day before the
Six-Day War. I'll never say
before the peace '45–'48 or during
the peace '56–'67.

But knowledge of peace
passes from country to country,
like children's games,
which are so much alive, everywhere.

18

The graves in Jerusalem are gates
of deep tunnels on the day of their opening –
after which they stop digging.

The tombstones are beautiful
cornerstones of buildings
that will never be built.

21

Jerusalem's a place where everyone remembers
he's forgotten something
but doesn't remember what it is.

And for the sake of remembering
I wear my father's face over mine.

This is the city where my dream containers fill up
like a diver's oxygen tanks.

Its holiness
sometimes turns into love.

And the questions that are asked in these hills
are the same as they've always been: 'Have you
seen my sheep?' 'Have you seen
my shepherd?'

And the door of my house stands open
like a tomb
where someone was resurrected.

22

This is the end of the landscape. Among blocks
of concrete and rusting iron
there's a fig tree with heavy fruit
but even kids don't come around to pick it.
This is the end of the landscape.
Inside the carcass of a mattress rotting in the field
the springs stay put, like souls.

The house I lived in gets farther and farther away
but a light was left burning in the window
so that people would only see and not hear.
This is the end.

And how to start loving again is like the problem
of architects in an old city: how to build
where houses once stood, so it will look like
those days, yet also like now.

23

Nineteen years this city was divided –
the lifetime of a young man who might have fallen in the
  war.
I long for the serenity and for the old longing.
Crazy people would cross through the fence that divided
  it,
enemies breached it,
lovers went up to it, testing,
like circus acrobats who try out the net
before they dare to jump.

The patches of no-man's-land were like placid bays,
longing floated overhead in the sky
like ships whose anchors stuck deep in us, and sweetly
  ached.

24

They are burning the photographs
of divided Jerusalem, and those
beautiful love letters of a silent love.

The big whole lady is back,
noisy with gold and copper and stones
for fat and legal life.

But I don't like her.
Sometimes I remember the quiet one.

25

An old gym teacher is broiling
in the sun by the wall. His shoes
are being shined far away

from his head. And high above,
longings stir like rustling paper.

I never realised gym teachers
could be sad. He is very tired
and wants nothing more than
that the beautiful tourist-girl sitting
beside him at a table will get up before him
and walk about with
her wobbling round buttocks,
which she has brought with her from her countries.
He wants nothing more.

29

People travel a long distance to be able to say: This
    reminds me of some other place.
It's like that time, it's similar. But
I knew a man who traveled all the way to New York
to commit suicide. He claimed that the buildings in
    Jerusalem
were too low and besides, everyone knew him here.

I remember him fondly because once
he called me out of the classroom in the middle of a
    lesson:
'A beautiful woman is waiting for you outside, in the
    garden.'
And he quieted the noisy children.

Whenever I think about the woman and the garden,
I remember him up on that high roof:
the loneliness of his death, the death of his loneliness.

32

In the lot through which lovers took a short cut
the Rumanian circus is parked.

Clouds mill around the setting sun like refugees
in a strange city of refuge.

A man of the twentieth century
casts a dark purple Byzantine shadow.

A woman shades her eyes with a raised hand, ringing
a bunch of lifted grapes.

Pain found me in the street
and whistled to his companions: Here's another one.

New houses flooded my father's grave
like tank columns. It stayed proud and didn't surrender.

A man who has no portion in the world to come
sleeps with a woman who does.

Their lust is reinforced by the self-restraint
in the monasteries all around.

This house has love carved on its gate
and loneliness for supports.

'From the roof you can see' or 'Next year' –
between these two a whole life goes on.

In this city, the water level
is always beneath the level of the dead.

33

A song of my homeland: The knowledge
of its waters starts with tears.

Sometimes I love water, sometimes stone.
These days I'm more in favour of stones.
But this might change.

34

Let the memorial hill remember instead of me,
that's what it's here for. Let the park in-memory-of
    remember,
let the street that's-named-for remember,
let the famous building remember,
let the synagogue that's named after God remember,
let the rolling Torah scroll remember, let the prayer
for the memory of the dead remember. Let the flags
    remember,
those multicolored shrouds of history: the bodies they
    wrapped
have long since turned to dust. Let the dust remember.
Let the dung remember at the gate. Let the afterbirth
    remember.
Let the beasts of the field and the birds of the heavens
eat and remember.
Let all of them remember so that I can rest.

35

In summer, peoples of different nations
visit each other
to smell out
each other's weak, sweet spots.

Hebrew and Arabic,
which are like stones of the tongue and sand of the
    throat,
have softened for tourists like oil.

Jeehad and holy wars
burst like figs.
Water pipes of Jerusalem protrude
like veins and tendons of an old, tired man.

Its houses are like teeth in the lower jaws
grinding in vain,
because heavens are empty above.

Perhaps Jerusalem is a dead city
in which people
swarm like maggots.

Sometimes they celebrate.

36

Every evening God takes his glittery merchandise
out of the shop window:
chariot works, tablets of law, fancy beads,
crosses and gleaming bells,
and puts them back into dark boxes
inside, and closes the shutter: 'Another day,
and still not one prophet has come to buy.'

37

All these stones, all this sorrow, all this
light, rubble of night hours and noon-dust,
all the twisted pipework of sanctity,
Wailing Wall, towers, rusty halos,
all the prophecies that – like old men – couldn't hold it in,
all the sweaty angels' wings,
all the stinking candles, all the prosthetic tourism,
dung of deliverance, bliss-and-balls,
dregs of nothingness, bomb and time.

All this dust, all these bones
in the process of resurrection and of the wind,
all this love, all these
stones, all this sorrow –

Go heap them into the valleys all around
so Jerusalem will be level
for my sweet airplane
that will come and carry me up.

[YA / TH: 1, 2, 3, 4, 5, 7, 8, 10, 11, 15, 18, 24, 25, 33, 35; CB: 21, 22, 23, 29, 32, 34, 36, 37]

Out of Three or Four in a Room

Out of three or four in a room
One is always standing at the window.
Forced to see the injustice amongst the thorns,
The fires on the hill.

And people who left whole
Are brought home in the evening, like small change.

Out of three or four in a room
One is always standing at the window.
Hair dark above his thoughts.
Behind him, the words.
And in front of him the words, wandering, without
    luggage.
Hearts without provision, prophecies without water
And big stones put there
And staying, closed, like letters
With no addresses; and no one to receive them.

[AG / TH]

88

Love Song II

People use each other
as a healing for their pain. They put each other
on their existential wounds,
on the eye, on the cunt, on mouth and open hand.
They hold each other hard and won't let go.

[YA / TH]

For Ever and Ever, Sweet Distortions

Pictures of dead Jews on the wall of a room in Petah
  Tikva,
Like stars that died eons ago
Whose light has only just reached us.

What's Jewish time? God's experimental places
Where he tests new ideas and new weaponry,
Training-ground for his angels and demons.
A red flag warns: Firing range!

What's the Jewish people? The quota that can be killed in
  training,
That's the Jewish people,
Which has not yet grown up, like a child that still uses the
Baby talk of its first years,
And still can't say
God's real name but says *Elohim*, *Hashem*, *Adonai*,
Dada, Gaga, Yaya, for ever and ever, sweet distortions.

[GA / TP]

Free

She is free. Free from the body
And free from the soul and from the blood that is the
    soul,
Free from wishes and from sudden fear
And from fear for me, free from honor and from shame
Free from hope and from despair and from fire and from
    water,
Free from the color of her eyes and from the color of her
    hair,
Free from furniture and free from knife spoon fork,
Free from the heavenly Jerusalem and from the earthly
    Jerusalem,
Free from identity and from identity documents,
Free from round seals
And from square seals,
Free from photos and free from clips,
She is free.

And all the letters and all the numbers
That arranged her life are free too
For new combinations and new destinies and new games
Of all the generations that will come after her.

    [BH / BH]

Tourist

She showed me her swaying hair
In the four winds of her coming.
I showed her some of my folding ways of life
And the trick, and the lock.
She asked after my street and my house

90

And I laughed loudly.
She showed me this long night
And the interior of her thirty years.
I showed her the place where I once laid *tefillin*.

I brought her chapters and verses
And sand from Eilat
And the handing of the Torah
And the manna of my death
And all the miracles that have not yet healed in me.

She showed me the stages of joy
And my childhood's double.
I revealed to her that King David is not buried in his tomb
And that I don't live in my life.
While I was reflecting and she was eating,
The city map lay open on the table –
Her hand on Qatamon
My hand on hers –
The cup covered the Old City,
Ash dropped on the King David Hotel,
And an ancient weeping
Allowed us to lie together.

[AG / TH]

Tourists

Visits of condolence is all we get from them.
They squat at the Holocaust Memorial,
They put on grave faces at the Wailing Wall
And they laugh behind heavy curtains
In their hotels.
They have their pictures taken

Together with our famous dead
At Rachel's Tomb and Herzl's Tomb
And on the top of Ammunition Hill.
They weep over our sweet boys
And lust over our tough girls
And hang up their underwear
To dry quickly
In cool, blue bathrooms.

Once I sat on the steps by a gate at David's Tower, I placed my two heavy baskets at my side. A group of tourists was standing around their guide and I became their target marker. 'You see that man with the baskets? Just right of his head there's an arch from the Roman period. Just right of his head.' 'But he's moving, he's moving!' I said to myself: redemption will come only if their guide tells them, 'You see that arch from the Roman period? It's not important: but next to it, left and down a bit, there sits a man who's bought fruit and vegetables for his family.'

[GA / TP]

Ibn Gabirol

Sometimes pus
Sometimes a poem.

Something always bursts out
And always pain.

My father was a tree in a forest of fathers
Covered in green cotton wool.

Oh, widows of the flesh, orphans of the blood,
I must escape.

Eyes sharp as tin-openers
Opened heavy secrets.

But through the wound on my chest
God peers into the world.

I am the door
To his apartment.

[AG / TH]

They Call Me

Taxis below
And angels above
Are impatient.
At one and the same time
They call me
With a terrible voice.

I'm coming, I am
Coming,
I'm coming down,
I'm coming up!

[AG / TH]

Jerusalem Ecology

The air above Jerusalem is saturated with prayers and
    dreams.
Like the air above industrial towns
it's hard to breathe.

And from time to time a new consignment of history
    arrives
And the houses and towers themselves are its packaging
Which is then thrown away and piled in heaps.

And sometimes candles come instead of men
And then silence.
And sometimes men come instead of candles
And then noise.

And in closed gardens, scented with jasmine,
Stand foreign consulates
Like evil brides that have been rejected,
Lying in wait for their moment.

[GA / TP]

The Bull Comes Home

The bull comes home from his workday in the ring
After drinking coffee with his fighters
And leaving them a note with his exact address
And the place of the red handkerchief.
(The sword stays stuck in his stiff-necked neck. And it
    stays.)
And he's at home now
And sitting on his bed, with his heavy

Jewish eyes. He knows
It hurts the sword too, when it plunges into flesh.
In the next reincarnation he'll be a sword:
The hurt will stay.
('The door
Is open. If not, the key is under the mat.')
He knows the mercy of evening
And true mercy. In the Bible
He is listed with the clean animals.
He is very kosher, chews his cud
And even his heart's divided and cleft
Like a hoof.
Out through his breast break hairs
Dry and grey as from a split mattress.

[HS]

The Diameter of the Bomb

The diameter of the bomb was thirty centimeters
and the diameter of its effective
range – about seven meters.
And in it four dead and eleven wounded.
And around them in a greater circle
of pain and time are scattered
two hospitals and one cemetery.
But the young woman who was
buried where she came from
over a hundred kilometers away
enlarges the circle greatly.
And the lone man who weeps over her death
in a far corner of a distant country
includes the whole world in the circle.

And I won't speak at all about the crying of orphans
that reaches to the seat of God
and from there onward, making
the circle without end and without God.

[YA / TH]

High-heeled Shoes

The earth answered several times:
Come in!
When you crossed the road in your tapping
High-heeled shoes,
It said, Come in!
But you couldn't hear.

[AG / TH]

Quick and Bitter

The end was quick and bitter.
Slow and sweet was the time between us,
Slow and sweet were the nights
When my hands did not touch one another in despair
But with the love of your body
Which came between them.

And when I entered into you
It seemed then that great happiness
Could be measured with the precision
Of sharp pain. Quick and bitter.

Slow and sweet were the nights.
Now is as bitter and grinding as sand –
'We shall be sensible' and similar curses.

And as we stray further from love
We multiply the words,
Words and sentences long and orderly.
Had we remained together
We could have become a silence.

[AG / TH]

The Figure of a Jewish Father

The figure of a Jewish father I am
with a sack on my back returning
home from the market. I have a rifle hidden
among soft woman-things in the closet in the scent of
    lingerie.
A man hit by the past and ill with future I am.
The fever of the present in his reddened eyes
unpaid and in vain he stands guard against evil.
Useless he guards against death,
guarding Jewish flesh, sweet like
all hunted flesh in agony. And at evening
he hears church bells rejoicing at the plight of Jews.
And from the hills a sad maneuver of brigades
with guns that have roots instead of wheels.
And he buys himself cream
for his cracked boots and his cracked lips.
And he smears it on for healing and for peace.

And he has documents of mercy and
papers of love in his coat.

And he sees people in their haste hurrying from past into
    future.
And at night, lonely and slowly he cooks jam,
stirring round and round till it grows pulpy and dense
with thick bubbles like thick Jewish eyes
and froth, white and sweet for coming generations.

[YA / TH]

The United Nations Command in Jerusalem

The mediators, the peace-makers, the compromisers, the
    pacifiers,
Live in the white house
And receive their nourishment from far away,
Through twisting channels, through dark veins, like a
    foetus.

And their secretaries are lipsticked and laughing,
And their immune chauffeurs wait below, like horses in a
    stable,
And the trees whose shadow shades them, have their
    roots in disputed territory,
And the delusions are children who go out into the fields
    to find cyclamen
And do not come back.

And the thoughts circle above, uneasily like scout-
    planes,
And they take photographs, and return, and develop the
    film
In dark, sad rooms.

And I know that they have very heavy chandeliers,
And the boy that I was sits on them and swings
In and out, in and out, and out, and does not come back.

Later on, the night will bring
Rusty and crooked conclusions out of our ancient lives
And above all the houses, the music
Will gather all the scattered things
Like a hand gathering crumbs off the table
After the meal, while the talk continues
And the children are already asleep.

And hopes come to me like daring sailors
Like discoverers of continents
To an island
And they rest for a day or two,
And then they sail away.

[AG / TH]

The Precision of Pain and the Blurriness of Joy

The precision of pain and the blurriness of joy. I'm
   thinking
how precise people are when they describe their pain in a
   doctor's office.
Even those who haven't learned to read and write are
   precise:
This one's a throbbing pain, and this one's
a wrenching pain, and this one gnaws, this one burns and
this is a sharp pain and this
is a dull one. Right here. Precisely here, yes, yes.
Joy blurs everything. I've heard people say
after nights of love and feasting, It was great,

99

I was in seventh heaven. And even the space man who floated
in outer space, tethered to a space ship, could only say, Great,
wonderful, I have no words.
The blurriness of joy and the precision of pain –
I want to describe with a sharp pain's precision
happiness and blurry joy. I learned to speak among the pains.

[CB / CK]

At the University of New Orleans

The quiet man showed me around campus,
His dead wife accompanied us, pleasant as heaven.
Girls lying on the lawn, God lying in heaven.

In this pretty place, between the fragrant flowerbeds,
The luxurious library building is meaningless.
Libraries are like orphanages,
The books stand there still, in straight lines,
The parents of the words died long ago.
And all that happened, as if it never happened.
History is the transmission of great weariness
To new, fresh people, like the girls
Sunbathing here almost naked in the grass,
Waiting for sunset
To make them even more beautiful.

[BH / BH]

Six Poems for Tamar

1

The rain is speaking quietly,
you can sleep now.

Near my bed, the rustle of newspaper wings.
There are no other angels.

I'll wake up early and bribe the coming day
to be kind to us.

2

You had a laughter of grapes:
many round green laughs.

Your body is full of lizards.
All of them love the sun.

Flowers grew in the field, grass grew on my cheeks
everything was possible.

3

You're always lying on
my eyes.

Every day of our life together
Ecclesiastes cancels a line of his book.

We are the saving evidence in the terrible trial.
We'll acquit them all!

4

Like the taste of blood in the mouth,
spring was upon us – suddenly.

The world is awake tonight.
It is lying on its back, with its eyes open:

The crescent moon fits the line of your cheek,
your breast fits the line of my cheek.

5

Your heart plays blood-catch
inside your veins.

Your eyes are still warm, like beds
time has slept in.

Your thighs are two sweet yesterdays,
I'm coming to you.

All hundred and fifty psalms
roar halleluyah.

6

My eyes want to flow into each other
like two neighboring lakes.

To tell each other
everything they've seen.

My blood has many relatives.
They never visit.

But when they die,
my blood will inherit.

[sm]

The Real Hero

The real hero of the Isaac story was the ram,
who didn't know about the conspiracy between the
    others.
As if he had volunteered to die instead of Isaac.
I want to sing a song in his memory –
about his curly wool and his human eyes,
about the horns that were so silent on his living head,
and how they made those horns into shofars when he was
    slaughtered
to sound their battle cries
or to blare out their obscene joy.

I want to remember the last frame
like a photo in an elegant fashion magazine:
the young man tanned and manicured in his jazzy suit
and beside him the angel, dressed for a party
in a long silk gown,
both of them empty-eyed, looking
at two empty places,

and behind them, like a colored backdrop, the ram,
caught in the thicket before the slaughter.
The thicket was his last friend.

The angel went home.
Isaac went home.
Abraham and God had gone long before.

But the real hero of the Isaac story
was the ram.

[CB]

Yehuda Ha-Levi

The soft hairs on the back of his neck
are the roots of his eyes.

His curly hair is
the sequel to his dreams.

His forehead: a sail; his arms: oars
to carry the soul inside his body to Jerusalem.

But in the white fist of his brain
He holds the black seeds of his happy childhood.

When he reaches the beloved, bone-dry land –
he will sow.

[SM]

Ballad of the Washed Hair

The stones on the mountain are always
awake and white.

In the dark town, angels on duty
are changing shifts.

A girl who has washed her hair
asks the hard world, as if it were Samson,
where is it weak, what is its secret.

A girl who has washed her hair
puts new clouds on her head.

The scent of her drying hair is
prophesying in the streets and among stars.

The nervous air between the night trees
starts to relax.

The thick telephone book of world history
closes.

[SM]

The Way a Photographer

The way a photographer, when he's composing a shot of
an ocean or a desert up to the edge of the horizon
and he has to get something large and near into the
    picture,
a branch, a chair, a boulder, the corner of a house
in order to sense the infinite, and he forgets the ocean
and the desert – that's how I love you, your hand,
your face, your hair, your nearby voice,
and I forget the everlasting distance and the endless
    endings.
And when we die, there will again be only the ocean and
    desert and God
we so much loved to look at from the window.
Farewell to the far and the near, to the true Gods, farewell.

[CB / CK]

Farewell to the far and the near: cf. Isaiah 57:19. The Hebrew *elohim*
is plural in form, and can mean either God or gods. In this context,
the Hebrew *shalom* can mean 'peace' as well as 'farewell'.

There are Many Grapes this Year

There are many grapes this year
but there is no peace in my heart. I eat them
Like a mad bird among scarecrows.

A smell of the last fruit has become
a smell of wine
that no one drinks. Big, black
grapes have turned my mouth
into a woman's insides.
Your lips discovered a ripe fig;
they'll stay that way through winter.
People interpreted bright landscapes
of summer's end, but I was thinking
about my love, which will not suffice
to cover this big land.

It has been a long year, filled
with fruit and the dead.
We wait for rain more than ever.
There are many grapes this year; the last are
yellow like the color of wild wasps
which are their death from within.

[HS]

Sadness of the Eyes and Descriptions of a Journey

There is a dark memory on which the noise of
Playing children is scattered like powdered sugar.

There are things which will never again
Protect you and there are doors stronger than tombs.

There is a melody like the one in Ma'adi,
Near Cairo – with a promise of things
Which the silence of now
Tries to keep, in vain.

And there is a place to which you can never return.
A tree hides it during the day
And a lamp lights it up at night.
And I can't say any more
And I don't know anything else.

To forget and blossom, to blossom and forget, is all.
The rest is sadness of the eyes and descriptions of a
　　journey.

[YA / TH]

Relativity

There's a toy ship with waves painted on it.
And there's a dress with sailing ships printed on it.
And there's the effort of remembering and the effort of
　　blooming
And there's the ease of love and the ease of death.
A dog of four years equals a man of thirty-five,
And a day-old fly – a man advanced in years
And full of memories. Three hours of thought
Are as two minutes of laughter,
And a child crying gives his hiding place away in the
　　game
And a silent child is forgotten.
Black long ago stopped being the color of mourning:
A girl squeezes herself into a black bikini
Cheekily.

A picture of a volcano on the wall
Soothes the people sitting in the room.
And a cemetery calms
By the quantity of its dead.

A man told me
That he's going down to Sinai because
He wants to be alone with his God:
I warned him.

[GA / TP]

A Pity, We Were Such a Good Invention

They amputated
Your thighs off my hips.
As far as I'm concerned
They are all surgeons. All of them.

They dismantled us
Each from the other.
As far as I'm concerned
They are all engineers. All of them.

A pity. We were such a good
And loving invention.
An airplane made from a man and wife.
Wings and everything.
We hovered a little above the earth.

We even flew a little.

[AG / TH]

King Saul and I

They gave him a finger, but he took the whole hand
They gave me the whole hand: I didn't even take the little
    finger.
While my heart
Was weightlifting its first feelings
He rehearsed the tearing of oxen.

My pulse-beats were like
Drips from a tap
His pulse-beats
Pounded like hammers on a new building.

He was my big brother
I got his used clothes.

2

His head, like a compass, will always bring him
To the sure north of his future.

His heart is set, like an alarm clock
For the hour of his reign.
When everyone's asleep, he will cry out
Until all the quarries are hoarse.
Nobody will stop him!

Only the asses bare their yellow teeth
At the end.

3

Dead prophets turned time-wheels
When he went out searching for asses
Which I, now, have found.
But I don't know how to handle them.
They kick me.

I was raised with straw,
I fell with heavy seeds.
But he breathed the winds of his histories.
He was anointed with the royal oil
As with wrestler's grease.
He battled with olive-trees
Forcing them to kneel.

Roots bulged on the earth's forehead
With the strain.
The prophets escaped from the arena;
Only God remained counting:
Seven . . . eight . . . nine . . . ten . . .
The people, from his shoulders downwards, rejoiced.
Not a man stood up.
He had won.

4

I am tired,
My bed is my kingdom.

My sleep is just
My dream is my verdict.

I hung my clothes on a chair
For tomorrow.

He hung his kingdom
In a frame of golden wrath
On the sky's wall.

My arms are short, like string too short
To tie a parcel.

His arms are like the chains in a harbour
For cargo to be carried across time.

He is a dead king.
I am a tired man.

[AG / TH]

To My Love

To my love, while combing her hair
without a mirror, facing me,
a psalm: You've washed your hair
with shampoo: A whole pine forest
breathes on your head in nostalgia.

Calmness from inside and calmness from outside
have hammered your face
between them like copper.

The pillow on your bed is your auxiliary brain
folded under your neck for memory and dream.

The earth trembles beneath us, my love.
Let's lie together, a double safety lock.

[YA / TH]

Letter

To sit on the veranda of a hotel in Jerusalem
and to write: Sweetly pass the days
from desert to sea. And to write: Tears, here,
dry quickly. This little blot
is a tear that has melted ink. That's how
they wrote a hundred years ago. 'I have
drawn a circle round it.'

Time passes – like somebody who, on a telephone,
is laughing or weeping far away from me:
whatever I'm hearing I can't see.
And whatever I see I don't hear.

We were not careful when we said 'next year'
or 'a month ago'. These words are like
glass splinters, which you can hurt yourself with,
or cut veins. Those who do things like that.

But you were beautiful, like the interpretation
of ancient books.
Surplus of women in your far country
brought you to me, but
other statistics have taken you
away from me.

To live is to build a ship and a harbor
at the same time. And to complete the harbor
long after the ship was drowned.

And to finish: I remember only
that there was mist. And whoever
remembers only mist –
what does he remember?

[YA / TH]

Ideal Love

To start love like this: with the shot of a gun
Like Ramadan.
That's a religion! Or with the blowing of a ram's horn,
As at the High Holidays, to exorcise sins.
That's a religion! That's a love!

Souls – to the front!
To the firing line of eyes.
No hiding back in the white navel.
Emotions – out of the fat belly, forward!
Emotions out for close combat!

But let's keep the route to childhood open –
As even the most victorious army
Always leaves itself a retreat open.

[YA / TH]

Ramadan: the Moslem month of fasting.

Too Many

Too many olive trees in the valley,
too many stones on the slope.
Too many dead, too little
earth to cover them all.
And I must return to the landscapes painted
on the bank notes
and to my father's face on coins.

Too many memorial days, too little
remembering. My friends have
forgotten what they learned when they were young.

And my girlfriend lies in a hidden place
and I am always outside, food for hungry winds.
Too much weariness, too few eyes
to contain it. Too many clocks,
too little time. Too many oaths
on the Bible, too many highways, too few
ways where we can truly go: each to his destiny.
Too many hopes
that ran away from their masters.
Too many dreamers. Too few dreams
whose interpretation would change the history of the
  world
like Pharaoh's dreams.

My life closes behind me. And I am outside, a dog
for the cruel and blind wind that always
pushes at my back. I am well trained: I rise and sit
and wait to lead it through the streets
of my life, which could have been my true life.

[SM]

Two Fragments of the Population Explosion

Two fragments of the population explosion,
We met by chance. Tiny, torn fragments.
But with whole nights and shared sleep until dawn.

And what a beautiful house it was, like the House
of the Lord! You eat and drink
And remember only once a year to fast and lament.

We didn't know the melting power of tears
And the breaking power of laughter which grinds
Everything to dust.

Now we still can say: 'Half a week
Three full days, another four nights.'

How poor in years and even days
Are those about to part but how rich
They are in minutes and seconds.

[GA / TP]

We Did It

We did it in front of the mirror
And in the light. We did it in darkness,
In water, and in the high grass.

We did it in honour of man
And in honour of beast and in honour of God.
But they didn't want to know about us,
They'd already seen our sort.

We did it with imagination and colours,
With confusion of reddish hair and brown
And with difficult gladdening
Exercises. We did it
Like wheels and holy creatures
And with chariot-feats of prophets.
We did it six wings
And six legs
    But the heavens
Were hard above us
Like the earth of the summer beneath.

[HS]

from The Achziv Poems

7

What's it like to be a woman?
What's it like to feel
a vacancy between the legs, curiosity
under the skirt, in summer, in wind,
and chutzpa at the haunches?

A male has to live with that odd sack
between his legs. 'Where would you like
me to put it?' asked the tailor,
measuring my pants,
and didn't smile.

What's it like to have a whole voice,
that never broke?
To dress and undress   slitherly
slinkily   caressively
like wearing olive oil,
to anoint the body with lithe fabrics,
a silky something,
a murmuring nothing of peach or mauve?
A male dresses with crude gestures of
buckling and edgy undoing,
angles, bones and stabs in the air,
and the wind's entangled in his eyebrows.

What's it like to 'feel a woman'?
And your body dreams you.
What's it like to love me?

Remains of a woman on my body,
and signs of the male on yours
augur the hell

which awaits us
and our mutual death.

[HS]

All These Make a Dance Rhythm

When a man grows older, his life becomes less dependent
on the rhythms of time and its seasons. Darkness
    sometimes
falls right in the middle of an embrace
of two people at a window; or summer comes to an end
during a love affair, while the love goes on
into autumn; or a man dies suddenly in the middle of
    speaking
and his words remain there on either side; or the same
    rain
falls on the one who says goodbye and goes
and on the one who says it and stays; or a single thought
wanders through cities and villages and many countries
in the head of a man who is traveling.

All these make a strange
dance rhythm. But I don't know who's dancing to it
or who's calling the tune.

A while back, I found an old photo of myself
with a little girl who died long ago.
We were sitting together, hugging as children do,
in front of a wall where a pear tree stood: her one hand
on my shoulder, and the other one free, reaching out from
    the dead
to me, now.

And I knew that the hope of the dead is their past,
and God has taken it.

[CB]

Hike with a Woman

When after hours of walking
You discover suddenly
That the body of the woman stepping beside you
Wasn't meant
For travel and war,

And that her thighs have become heavy
And her buttocks move like a tired flock,
You swell with a great joy
For the world
In which women are like that.

[HS]

When I Banged My Head on the Door

When I banged my head on the door, I screamed,
'My head, my head,' and I screamed, 'Door, door,'
and I didn't scream 'Mama' and I didn't scream 'God'.
And I didn't prophesy a world at the End of Days
where there will be no more heads and doors.

When you stroked my head, I whispered,
'My head, my head,' and I whispered, 'Your hand, your
    hand,'
and I didn't whisper 'Mama' or 'God'.
And I didn't have miraculous visions

of hands stroking heads in the heavens
as they split wide open.

Whatever I scream or say or whisper is only
to console myself: My head, my head.
Door, door. Your hand, your hand.

[CB]

When I Die

When I die, I want only women to handle me in the
     Chevra Kadisha
and do with my body as they pretty please: cleanse my
     ears of the last words
I heard, wipe my lips of the last words I said,
erase the sights I saw from my eyes, smooth my brow of
     worries
and fold my arms across my chest like the sleeves of a
     shirt after ironing.
And salve my flesh with perfumed oil to anoint me King
     of Death for a day
and arrange in my pelvic basin as in a fruit bowl
testes and penis, navel and frizzy hair
like an ornate still life from some past century,
a very still life on a ground of dark velvet,
and tickle my mouth-hole and asshole with a feather to
     check,
Is he still alive?
And laugh and cry by turns and administer a last massage
so it passes from their hands through me to the entire
     world
till the End of Days.
And one of them will sing *God Full of Mercy*,

will sing in a sweet voice *Merciful Womb*,
to remind God that mercy is born from the womb, true
    mercy,
true womb, true love, true grace.
On my life, that's what I want in my death, in my life, on
    my life.

[CB / CK]

Chevra Kadisha (lit., The Sacred Fellowship): a group of Orthodox
males who fulfil the sacred duty of preparing the dead body for burial.
Women are not permitted by rabbinic law to be members of this
group, though they prepare women's bodies for burial. In Israel, where
there is no separation of church and state, the *Chevra Kadisha*
controls all funeral practices.
    God Full of Mercy (Hebrew: *El Male Rahamim*): the funeral prayer.
'Grant perfect rest beneath the wings of thy Divine Presence.' 'Womb'
(Hebrew: *rehem*) in the next line has the same root letters as 'mercy'
(*rahamim*).

When I was Young the Whole Country was Young

When I was young, the whole country was young. And
    my father
was everyone's father. When I was happy, the country
was happy too, and when I jumped on her, she jumped
under me. The grass that covered her in spring
softened me too, and the dry earth of summer hurt me
like my own cracked footsoles.
When I first fell in love, they proclaimed
her independence, and when my hair
fluttered in the breeze, so did her flags.
When I fought in the war, she fought, when I got up
she got up too, and when I sank
she began to sink with me.

Now I'm beginning to come apart from all that:
like something that's glued, after the glue dries out,
I'm getting detached and curling into myself.

The other day I saw a clarinet player in the Police Band
that was playing at David's Citadel.
His hair was white and his face calm: a face
of 1946, the one and only year
between famous and terrible years
when nothing happened except for a great hope and his
    music
and my loving a girl in a quiet room in Jerusalem.
I hadn't seen him since then, but the hope for a better
    world
never left his face.

Afterward I bought myself some non-kosher salami
and two bagels, and I walked home.
I managed to hear the evening news
and ate and lay down on the bed
and the memory of my first love came back to me
like the sensation of falling
just before sleep.

[CB]

Outing at Some Beautiful Place

With a Jewish girl
Who has American hope
In her eyes and whose nostrils are still
Very sensitive to anti-Semitism.

'Where did you get those eyes?'
Eyes like those one does not receive at birth –
So much color, so much sadness.

She wore the coat of a soldier, discharged
Or dead – by victory or defeat –
In some worn-out war.

'On a bonfire of burned letters
It is impossible to cook even one cup of coffee.'

After that to continue walking
To some beautiful, hidden place
At which a wise and experienced field commander
Would have put his mortars.

'In the summer, after you, this hill
Gets covered by a soft thought.'

[YA / TH]

You Carry the Load

You carry the load of heavy buttocks,
but your eyes are clear.
Around your waist you wear a strong belt
which won't be able to protect you.

You are made of material that slows down
the process of joy and its pain.

I have already taught my penis
to say your name, like a clever bird.
You seem unimpressed by this,
you pretend not to hear it.
What else should I have done for you?

Now all that's left to me
is your name
which has become completely independent, like an
    animal:
It eats out of my hand and
lies down at night
curled up in my dark brain.

[YA / TH]

Inside the Apple

You visit me inside the apple
Together we can hear the knife
paring around and around us, carefully,
so the peel won't tear.

You speak to me. I trust your voice
because it has lumps of hard pain in it
the way real honey
has lumps of wax from the honeycomb.

I touch your lips with my fingers:
that too is a prophetic gesture.
And your lips are red, the way a burnt field
is black.
It's all true.

You visit me inside the apple
and you'll stay with me inside the apple
until the knife finishes its work.

[CB]

National Thoughts

You: trapped in the homeland of the Chosen People.
On your head a cossack's fur hat,
Child of their pogroms.
'After these words.' Always.
Or, for instance, your face: slanting eyes,
Pogrom-Year eyes. Your cheekbones, high,
Hetman's cheekbones, Hetman the rabble-king.
Hassid dancing, dutiful, you, naked on a rock in the early
    evening by the canopies of water at Ein Geddi
With eyes closed and your body open like hair.

After these words, 'Always.'
Every day I know the miracle of
Jesus walking upon the waters,
I walk through my life without drowning.

To speak, now, in this tired language
Torn from its sleep in the Bible –
Blinded, it lurches from mouth to mouth –
The language which described God and the Miracles,
    Says:
Motor car, bomb, God.

The squared letters wanted to stay closed,
Every letter a locked house,
To stay and to sleep in it for ever.

[AG / TH]

124

Afterword DANIEL WEISSBORT

It was at a New Year's party (1963–4) that Ted Hughes mentioned to me his idea for a magazine devoted solely to poetry in translation. He had already discussed the possibility with various individuals in the United States, but had then returned to England. I was much taken with this thought and began to explore the international scene, so to speak. Ted himself was particularly drawn to some of the poetry of Eastern Europe that was becoming visible to us in the aftermath of the so-called Thaw following on Stalin's death in 1953 and spreading throughout the Soviet domain. Poets of the first post-War generation, such as the Poles Tadeusz Rozewicz, Zbigniew Herbert, the Czech Miroslav Holub and the Yugoslav Vasko Popa, most directly affected us. I began identifying translators and collecting translations; at the same time, I investigated other countries, including Israel. In this case, I wrote to Dennis Silk, an English poet living in Jerusalem, asking him quite simply and naively whether he could recommend some contemporary Israeli poets for a new magazine that Ted Hughes and I were thinking of starting. He wrote back recommending Yehuda Amichai above all and including several samples of the latter's work in translations by a number of hands. The first issue of *Modern Poetry in Translation*, thus, included work by Amichai, alongside translations of Herbert, Holub, Popa, as well as Ivan Lalic, Czeslaw Milosz and Andrei Voznesensky. Each poet was represented by a substantial enough selection and there was the barest biblio-biographical information, no criticism or commentary. Amichai's early translators included Dom Moraes, Margalit Benaya, Arieh Sachs, Abraham Birman and Dennis Silk himself.

In his Introduction to *Amen* (Harper & Row, 1977) Ted Hughes, who had co-translated the poems in that book with the author, referred to this initial issue of *MPT* and the Amichai poems in it. ('We were both greatly intrigued and excited by them,' he wrote.) I shall quote him here and below at length, since his introduction to *Amen* still seems to me the best general account of Yehuda Amichai's poetry.

[Amichai's poems] eventually appeared, in that first issue, in powerful company: Zbigniew Herbert, Miroslav Holub, Vasko Popa. These poets were the same generation as Amichai, early 1920s, and each one of them had some claim to being among the dozen most remarkable poets alive [. . .] It seemed to us that Amichai shared their stature and something of their family likeness. Nevertheless, he stood a little apart, and with the passing of time it has become clearer just how radically different he is. In 1966, it was already noticeable that where the three poets from behind the Iron Curtain gripped one's imagination and held one's awe, somehow Amichai's verse attracted and held one's affection as well. It became involved with one's intimate daily experience in a curious way.

Indeed, so intrigued was Ted Hughes by these poems that he collaborated with Assia Gutmann in the very first volume of Amichai's work in English (*Yehuda Amichai: Selected Poems*, Cape Goliard, 1968). These translations were later re-published by Penguin, along with other versions by Harold Schimmel. Ted Hughes did not comment on either the translations or the poet, the insightful introduction to the Penguin volume coming from Michael Hamburger. However, his (Hughes's) close-ness to Amichai is apparent from the start. Again, from his introduction to *Amen*: 'I am more than ever con-vinced that here is one kind of poetry that satisfies, for me, just about every requirement.'

Hughes's translations of Amichai inaugurated the remarkable series of translations that have come from his pen. Apart from Amichai, he translated (with Janos Csokits) another poet of the first post-War generation, the Hungarian Janos Pilinszky. Then there are his stage versions of Seneca, Racine, Wedekind, Lorca, Aeschylus, not to mention his (now staged) Ovid. And there was more promised, a stage version of Gilgamesh, transla-tions from the Anglo-Saxon, besides which there were many occasional translations, from Portuguese, Hungar-ian and probably other languages.

Much of Ted Hughes's translation work related to his abiding and many-faceted interest in drama, significant here being the work he did with Peter Brook in the early seventies. It was Brook, of course, who directed the Hughes version of Seneca's *Oedipus*. Later Ted Hughes worked with Brook's international group, inventing a language, 'Orghast', for the Shiraz Festival in Iran, in 1971. It is not surprising, then, that he describes Amichai's poetry in terms of a drama. Again, I quote at length:

> To appreciate what he manages to do, one has to imagine him as the chief character in a drama – chief in the sense that he is the one on whom we see the drama registering all its pressures. In this case, his speeches have the added authority that the role is real, and the drama is that crucial hinge of modern history – particularly the history of the West – which is the dilemma of modern Israel.

The forces on the move in this drama are for anybody to name. Even to such an outsider as myself, it is a matter of wonder to see such temperamental energies and traditions, from all the diverse corners of the diaspora, drawn back with the suddenness and violence of collision into that tiny patch of bare land, and there forced to combine and fight against what has repeatedly threatened to be not just defeat but extinction.

Every aspect of the situation is relevant to Amichai's poetry. The simplest assessment of the plot of the drama, and the dramatic personae, has to take account of the unique intensity of Jewish religious feeling, and its meaning for all Western Peoples. It has to take account of the Prophets, Biblical history, the supernatural world of Jewish mystical tradition, and the symbolic role of Israel itself, and in particular of Jerusalem. The accumulated inner strength and wealth of Jewish survival throughout the diaspora, and the peculiar election imposed on them by Hitler. The fact of the holocaust. The fact of the suddenly multiplying powers of the Arab world. A plot that enmeshes itself in a perpetual state of near-war, sudden wars, the threat of more and worse wars, endless future warfare while world powers shift the country this way and that like a pawn. It is clearly the drama of a war of survival on every level, the culmination of the long Jewish history of fighting for survival on every level, of a garrisoned last-stand people. At the same time, ironically, it is the story of a hectic modern Mediterranean holiday land, a tourist resort aswarm with nymphs and satyrs.

But this is only the start of the play. The plot now

requires that this huge problem of spiritual inheritance and immediate physical challenge be solved, or at least dealt with in a practical way. And the character on whom this task has descended, the inheritor, the responsible man, the Prince Hamlet, is the modern Israeli citizen-soldier. But is he up to the job? This hero is not a full-time philosopher or general. The weird unmanageable fate has fallen on the shoulders of a man in the street, probably a schoolteacher, a conscript in all the wars, an ordinary individual who also happens to be in love. And that is what concerns him most, that he is in love.

This character's love poems, as the drama lurches along all round him, have been written by Yehuda Amichai.

Ted Hughes's loyalty to Amichai, his identification with elements of the drama he perceived as embracing the latter's work, only grew with the years. As he put it, Amichai belonged to that great generation of East European poets but was somehow *different* – it is in that difference that Hughes found what he could love. He put it thus, trying to get at the translatability of Amichai as of his East European contemporaries like Holub, Herbert, Popa:

> The dramatic role which Amichai has had to perform obviously demands unusual linguistic resources, for any adequate expression. Luckily for us who cannot read the Hebrew, he did not rest content with purely verbal means. What he has in common with Herbert, Holub and Popa is a language beyond verbal language, a language of images which operates with the syntactical complexity and richness of hieroglyphs.

In his introduction to the first Poetry International, held in London in 1967 and directed by himself and Patrick Garland, Hughes had written:

> However rootedly-national in detail it may be, poetry is less and less the prisoner of its own language. It is beginning to represent, as an ambassador, something far greater than itself. Or perhaps it is only now being heard for what, among other things, it is – a Universal language of understanding, coherent behind the many languages, in which we can all hope to meet.

Reading these words today, over thirty years later, one is struck of course by their idealistic ring. Also, I think, by their visionary quality, as though Hughes had in mind an *ursprache*, a third language between source and target languages. Implicit was an emphatic denial of Robert Frost's much quoted remark that poetry was what got lost in translation. Of course, Ted Hughes's words were not to the liking of all, and one has to say that, to some extent, his views on the translatability of poetry were posited on the peculiar translatability precisely of the East European poets mentioned here, in whose numbers he and I would have included Yehuda Amichai.

But, as against this, even in seeming contradiction of it, he espoused a severely literalistic approach to verse translation. Indeed, the first issue of *MPT* made much of the desirability of remaining lexically close to the original. It was the opportunity for literal translation which, among other things, appealed to Hughes in the work of Popa, Holub, or Amichai. Their voices came through the least *literary* versions, with astonishing immediacy. In our joint editorial to *MPT* No. 1, we expressed these views. The words here are mostly Ted's:

The type of translations we are seeking can be described as literal, though not literal in a strict or pedantic sense. Though this may seem at first suspect, it is more apposite to define our criteria negatively, as literalness can only be a deliberate tendency, not a dogma. We feel that as soon as devices extraneous to the original are employed for the purpose of recreating its 'spirit', the value of the whole enterprise is called in question.

For some years Ted Hughes and I had thought of putting together a 'big Amichai', drawing on the works of his many translators. Apart from Hughes himself and Assia Gutmann, these include Stephen Mitchell, Ruth Nevo, Harold Schimmel, Chana Bloch and Chana Kronfeld, Glenda Abramson and Tudor Parfitt, Robert Friend, and Barbara and Benjamin Harshav. The fact that Amichai had been translated so often and by so many different translators was for us further indication that he belonged to all and had not become any single translator's private possession. We regarded it as altogether fitting that Amichai should be listened to in English, as relayed by diverse voices, even if it was also worth remembering that the poet himself had not infrequently had a hand in the translation process and that his own English versions (see Ted Hughes's remarks below) are remarkably persuasive. In the last year or so of Ted Hughes's life, the proposed comprehensive selection from Amichai's poetry in English translation occupied much of his attention. Since he knew how ill he was, this project clearly was of primary importance to him.

He and I read through all available translations and made our choices independently of one another. We then conferred and came up with a final list which we submitted to Christopher Reid at Faber and Faber. It was felt by the latter that the gathering was too large to be commercially feasible and that certain redundancies were apparent. We then went through it again, reducing it by about a third. In general, although Ted Hughes deferred to me quite often, I felt strongly that the final selection should represent, rather, his choice of Amichai's poetry. It was Hughes, too, who decided that rather than present the texts chronologically, we should place them in alphabetical order of first lines (a variation on the practice adopted for *The Rattlebag*, the anthology he co-edited with Seamus Heaney, in which the poems ran in alphabetical order of titles). This may seem to be avoiding a difficult task, but actually Amichai's work, which now can be viewed from the heights of a lifetime's achievement, is remarkably of a piece. The random arrangement underlines the coherence of his total oeuvre.

At one time, we thought of including one or two poems in several versions, or presenting in an appendix several drafts by Hughes himself of the same poem. However, when I consulted the Hughes archives, after his death, it became apparent that, as he claimed in his Introduction to *Amen*, he had indeed altered very little the drafts that Amichai made for him. (This was not the case with his translations of Janos Pilinszky, although he claimed there as well that he had done little to alter his co-translator Janos Csokits's literal versions.) I am reminded of a remark of Ted's, in an unattributed editorial to *Modern Poetry in Translation* (Spring 1967):

A man who has something really serious to say in a language of which he knows only a few words, manages to say it far more convincingly and effectively than any interpreter, and in translated poetry it is the first-hand contact – however fumbled and broken – with that man and his seriousness which we want. The minute we gloss his words, we have more or less what he said but we have lost him. We are ringing changes – amusing though they may be – on our own familiar abstractions, and are no longer reaching through to what we have not experienced before, which is alive and real.

Of course he did not have in mind Amichai, whose knowledge of English is far from 'fumbled and broken'. Nevertheless, what is evident is that Hughes listened to, cherished the voice within. In his translations of poetry, this is what he sought to preserve, to keep audible. His translations are acts of selfless love. Here, then, finally, is Ted Hughes on his co-translations of Amichai:

> The translations were made by the poet himself. All I did was correct the more intrusive oddities and errors of grammar and usage, and in some places shift about the phrasing and line endings. What I wanted to preserve above all was the tone and cadence of Amichai's own voice speaking in English, which seems to me marvellously true to the poetry, in these renderings. What Pound called the first of all poetic virtues – 'the heart's tone'. So as translations these are extremely literal. But they are also more, they are Yehuda Amichai's own English poems.

Of his own poetry, Amichai, asked to comment, wrote in that first issue of *Modern Poetry in Translation*:

> Yosef ben Matityahu (Josephus Flavius) was a field-commander of the Judaean Army in Galilee that

fought Vespasian and Titus. He went over to the Romans, and wrote the history of the campaign he had fought. He chose to write about what he had been involved in. I agree with Josephus. I want to be involved and avoid writing, and then to be detached and write. The debate continues as to whether Josephus was, or was not, a traitor.

This volume, then, is both a representative selection of Yehuda Amichai's poetry and the record of a friendship between two great poets of the twentieth century.

Acknowledgements

The editors and publishers gratefully acknowledge permission to use copyright material in this book as follows: poems translated by Glenda Abramson and Tudor Parfitt from *Great Tranquillity: Questions and Answers* (Harper & Row, 1983), by kind permission of HarperCollins; poems translated by Abraham Birman first printed in *Modern Poetry in Translation 1*; poems translated by Chana Bloch and Chana Kornfeldt from *Open Closed Open* (Harcourt Brace), by kind permission of Georges Borchardt, Inc. (the translations printed here are those sent to and selected by the editors of this volume, prior to their publication, often in revised versions, in *Open Closed Open*); poems translated by Robert Friend from *Love Poems* (Harper & Row, 1981), by kind permission of HarperCollins Publishers, Inc.; poems translated by Assia Gutmann (with the collaboration of Ted Hughes) and by Harold Schimmel (page 115) from *Selected Poems* (Jonathan Cape, 1971), by kind permission of Random House Archive and Library; poems translated by Benjamin and Barbara Hershev from *A Life of Poetry: 1948–1994* (HarperCollins, 1994), by kind permission of HarperCollins Publishers, Inc.; poems translated by Ted Hughes with the author (YA) from *Amen* (Oxford University Press, 1978) and *Times* (Oxford University Press, 1979), by kind permission of Oxford University Press; poems translated by Stephen Mitchell and by Chana Bloch (pages 3, 6, 8, 20, 23, 37, 38, 42, 47, 48, 54, 57, 59, 65, 66, 72, 75, 103, 117, 118, 120, 123) from *The Selected Poetry of Yehuda Amichai* (University of California Press, 1996), by kind permission of the University of California Press; poems translated by Harold Schimmel (pages 4, 13, 15, 22, 28, 31, 36, 57, 94, 106, 118) from *Songs of Jerusalem and Myself* (Harper & Row, 1973), by kind permission of HarperCollins; poems translated by Harold Schimmel (page 116) and by Dennis Silk from *Poems of Jerusalem and Love Poems* (Sheep Meadow Press), by kind permission of Sheep Meadow Press.

135